green /grēn/

adjective

• of the color between blue and yellow in the spectrum; colored like grass or emeralds: *the leaves are bright green.*

• covered with grass, trees, or other plants: *proposals that would smother green fields with development.*

noun

• green color or pigment: *recreation areas are marked in green.*

• a piece of public or common grassy land, especially in the center of a town: *a house overlooking the green.*

verb

• make or become green in color: *the roof was greening with lichen.*

• make less harmful or more sensitive to the environment: *the importance of greening this industry.*

Oxford English Dictionary, 3rd Edition

IN THIS ISSUE

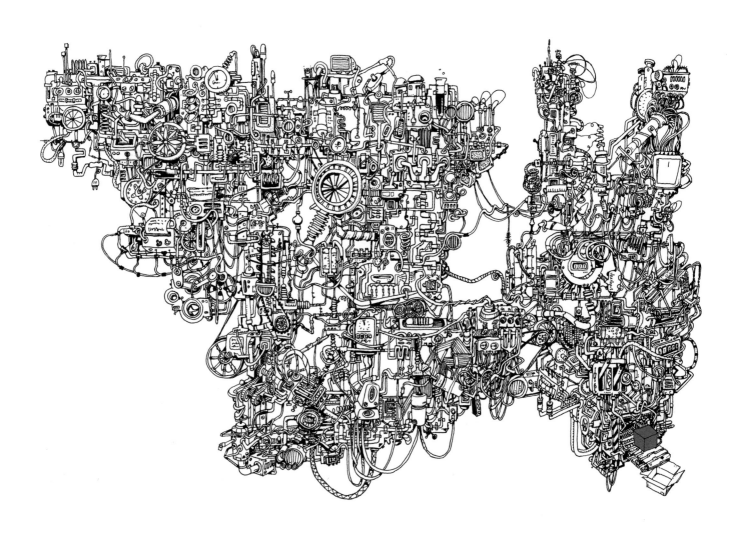

Above: *Green* (2020) by Georg Bautz.

LA+ GREEN
EDITORIAL

It's disturbing to think that the world has no intrinsic color. Colors are literally figments of our imaginations – an illusory effect of light bouncing off different materials at different wavelengths converted through our eyes and into our brains, where we give them names. If all the light hitting an object bounces off that object we call it white; if all the light is absorbed, we call it black. In between is the rainbow. But if color is a biophysical fabrication of our bodies, then it begs the question, what does the world actually look like? The first answer depends on who's looking; for example, where we see white, bees see ultra-violet. The second answer is reached by wondering, as Einstein did, what the world "looks" like to light itself. From that angle, everything is colorless, or perhaps in terms we can understand, a sort of grayish blur.

One of the great joys of being in a body is the experience of color and for this issue of LA+ we've chosen to focus on green. Why? Because, rightly or wrongly, of all the colors green is associated most with landscape. And also, because the word "green" has become synonymous with an ecological world view and, from the Green Parties of the 1980s to today's Green New Deal, a certain set of political aspirations. But above all, we just wanted to do an entire issue using color as a theme, and when we asked which color is most relevant to contemporary design culture, green shines through. To tee up the issue we invited Kassia St. Clair, author of *The Secret Lives of Colors* to provide us with a snapshot of how green has been variously valued by different cultures at different times.

When asked their favorite color, the most popular answer around the world is blue, and when thinking of our planet, most people will picture the famous "Blue Marble" photos of Earth from the Apollo space missions. But as the world urbanizes and blue skies fill with carbon, one wonders if green–the signature color of fecundity and plant life–will come to the fore. Two articles in this issue, one by urban designer Julian Bolleter with Cristina Ramalho and Robert Freestone, and the other by a team of environmental scientists led by Robert McDonald, argue for the significance of green space and trees in supporting dense yet livable cities. Historian Sonja Dümpelmann charts the history of planting design to identify the shifting status of the color green in comparison to other effects. Relatedly, Michael Geffel, Brian Osborn, and Julian Raxworthy explain their research into new ways of designing landscapes through novel maintenance regimes, and Parker Sutton considers ways in which plants, and landscapes more broadly, are [mis]represented in contemporary social media.

Picking up where Sutton leaves off, guru of contemporary media studies Shannon Mattern uses the green screen as her Ariadne's thread and wends her way through the work of a number of contemporary artists for whom the color plays an important role. Just as Mattern takes us beyond landscape architecture to other design practices, so too Richard Weller reviews four major exhibitions and argues that landscape architects have much to learn from how other designers, along with scientists and philosophers, are conceiving of a denatured world and the role of design within it. Speaking of philosophers, we are delighted to introduce Michael Marder to a design readership. Marder is quite probably the most important–and certainly the deepest–thinker regarding human-plant relationships in the world today.

Turning to green as a political and environmental moniker, we interview the doyen of international green socialism Noam Chomsky about his book *Climate Crisis and the Global Green New Deal*. We then check the whiteness of the recent history of environmentalism by interviewing Robert D. Bullard, also known as the "father of environmental justice," and Tamara Toles O'Laughlin, the first African American to lead a major environmental organization who has advocated a "Black climate agenda." Neil Maher, an authority on the history of the Civilian Conservation Corps, then explains how he thinks a Green New Deal could mobilize a new generation of labor while avoiding the racial pitfalls and other problems associated with the original New Deal. The issue of ecological restoration is then taken to a global scale as Rob Levinthal explores the Great Green Wall – the world's largest living megastructure being built across the African Sahel. Finally, just in case you should find yourself being seduced by green's seemingly infinite virtues, Peder Anker takes that paragon of ecological virtue, Norway, and exposes how its national image is a carefully greenwashed myth.

And so, it seems, it's really not that easy bein' green!

Richard Weller, Nicholas Pevzner + Tatum L. Hands
Issue Editors

Kassia St. Clair is a London-based writer and author of *The Secret Lives of Color* (2016) and *The Golden Thread: How Fabric Changed History* (2018). She holds an MA in history from Oxford University and writes about history, culture, and design for publications including *The Economist*, *Wired*, and the *Times Literary Supplement*. She is currently writing a book about an improbable early-20th-century automobile journey from Peking to Paris.

✚ HISTORY, ART

Opposite: Georg Friedrich Kersting, *Embroidery Woman* (1817), painted using Scheele's Green.

KASSIA ST. CLAIR
THE COLOR OF YEARNING

Wassily Kandinsky, who boasted an array of strong opinions on colors, was rather ambivalent about green. While he believed it was "the most restful color that exists," he also thought it passive, wearisome, and "'bourgeoisie' – self-satisfied, immovable, narrow."[1] His naked distaste is jarring. Humans are more usually to be found struggling toward green rather than shying away from it. It is valued and valuable. We miss it when it is gone. It is a color that is seemingly perpetually, tantalizingly, right there. At the tips of our fingers. All too often just out of reach.

Although nature and the natural world is conspicuously multi-hued it has long been symbolically aligned with green.[2] But this seemingly instinctive association between nature and green is not surprising: we have depended on greenery for food and grazing from the earliest days of our species. We seek it out, thriving in places with regular growing seasons. During colder, drier months we await the signs that spring is on its way: veils of green stealthily drawn over fields and hedgerows. The tender green of buds, sprouts, shoots, and tips all of a sudden alive and awake and pushing their way up and toward the light.

Chlorophyll—the pigment in plants responsible both for their color and their ability to harness energy through photosynthesis—is the bedrock of the food chain. In addition to food, plants give us shelter. They can be used to build walls and thatch roofs. Some, like cotton and flax, can be used to create textiles with which we make nets, string, and rope, or clothes to protect our delicate bodies. From others we can produce dyes of almost any tint imaginable (although, strangely enough, these dyes seem very rarely to be green). Plants can also be used to produce paper, the medium on which we record our thoughts, our lives, our creations. Green, then, can stand in for life itself.

The human yearning for and dependence on green is also embedded in language. The ancient Egyptians' hieroglyph for this color, for example, depicted a papyrus frond, a beloved and supremely useful plant, and it was further associated with positive attributes, including fertility and rebirth. The English word, like its German cousin *grün*, springs from the same Proto-Indo-European root: ghrē-, to grow. Similarly, *vert* (French) and *verde* (Spanish and Italian) share a Latin ancestor, *viridis*, which was related to *virere*, to "be green," and gave the English tongue the words verdure, viridian, and verdant.

Although its opposite on color wheels is red, it is fascinating how often writers and philosophers contrast green with grey. The English poet Algernon Swinburne wrote of "Green pleasure or grey grief."[3] For Johann von Goethe it was theory that was grey, while "actual life springs ever green."[4] Culturally, it has also been the rural to grey's urban; the growth to its withering. Kandinsky, funnily enough, wrote that a "silent and motionless" grey could be "produced by a mixture of green and red, a spiritual blend of passivity and glowing warmth."[5]

Still, green spaces and surroundings are clearly important to us. The idea that green soothes the eyes is an old one: Virgil, Pliny, and other Roman writers mention it. Indeed, crushed emeralds were said to make efficacious eye balms. More practically, the meditative exposure to woodland spaces, known as *shinrin-yoku* or forest bathing, has been an official part of Japan's national health program since the early 1980s. Other countries have followed suit. Some $4 million were spent in the decade after 2004 researching the potential health benefits of access to green spaces and the results have been encouraging. A study by King's College in London, for example, showed that mindful time in green spaces could reduce cortisol levels and blood pressure.[6]

Green enclosures in the form of manicured gardens loom large in our imagination, particularly when it comes to picturing pleasure, salvation, and paradise. The Ancient Greek pantheon frequented sacred groves, lush pastures, and orchards. True believers, according to the Qur'an, are promised "gardens, beneath which rivers flow, wherein they abide eternally, and pleasant dwellings in gardens of perpetual residence."[7] Green is also inextricably linked in Islam with Muhammed, who is believed to have worn green clothing in life and, after his death, to have been covered with yet more green cloth. Christians, for their part, have the Garden of Eden, the fecund paradise from which Adam and Eve, the first humans, were expelled in shame after sampling the forbidden fruit.

Naturally enough, those on earth have sought to recreate such heavenly spaces in the physical realm. The earliest earthly paradise is thought to have appeared in what is now southern Iraq around 5,000 BCE when irrigation techniques allowed people to transfigure the desert into a leafier, greener land. Nearby, several millennia later, the Hanging Gardens of Babylon–known as one of the Seven Wonders of the World– were laid out and carefully tended. Gardens like these were created as a show of wealth (they required time, patience, and money to perfect), but also as locations in which to socialize. Those who tend their equivalents today are said to possess green fingers or thumbs.

Green spaces like gardens, woods, and forests make for ideal dramatic and literary settings, offering ample opportunities for private trysts, public displays, hunting, and feasting. Rigid social norms, relatively easy to police inside, loosen like untied stays once turned outside into the fresh air and verdure. During the Middle Ages, this was formalized by the French court, which

on the first day of May encouraged *s'esmayer*, or "wearing of May." This meant courtiers dressing in green, or donning crowns or necklaces of leaves and flowers, and then parading and participating in expressions of courtly love.

As well as delighting in cultivating exterior gardens, it has been common for centuries to draw elements of the greenery outside into our interiors. William Morris's dense foliate designs immediately spring to mind, but styled tendrils, shoots, branches, fruit, flowers, and vines are foundational elements and motifs in almost all the decorative languages humans have built up. Romans, to pluck one example, delighted in vegetative decorations. The Villa of Livia, situated just north of Rome, was decorated around 20 BCE with extraordinary frescoes of garden views. And, in 16th-century Sussex, England, an inventory of Arundel Castle conjures a home swathed in leafy green, from carpets and curtains to "verdures" – tapestries depicting woodland scenes.

It is perhaps apt here to introduce green's darker side. After all gardens, if left untamed, shade into wilderness, which, while not exclusively hostile, certainly have their perils. Green spaces are often filled with complex, obscuring shadows. Piquant delights may lurk under green canopies, but so too do sins and terrors: poison, avarice, jealousy–Shakespeare's "greene-ey'd Monster"–and, of course, the devil and his creatures, foremost among them the biblical serpent, forked tongue vibrant against glossy emerald skin.

Even green's most ardent admirers have found it ephemeral. Green passions–whether negative like greed or positive like youthful love–often burn out quickly, leaving the sufferer off balance and humiliated. Green colorants have proved equally inconstant. Those tapestries on Arundel Castle's walls probably owed their color to two dye baths, the first one blue and the second yellow. Over time, and with exposure to sunlight, the yellows were wont to fade and disappear, the foliage turning wan shades of teal and cerulean.

For artists, pure green options are limited. Earth green or *terre verte*–a naturally occurring mixture of clay and iron silicate– is a reliably cheap pigment. But, although soft, buttery, and easy to use, it discolors over time and is usually rather dull in tone. For something more vibrant, artists struggled with greens procured from copper, such as verdigris, which appears on copper exposed to salt, water, and air – like the sea-foam crust that adorns the Statue of Liberty. Verdigris has been purposely produced as a pigment since at least the 4th century BCE by exposing sheets of copper to something containing acetic acid, usually wine or vinegar. The resulting green pigment was relatively saturated, but Leonardo da Vinci warned that verdigris "loses its beauty like smoke if it is not quickly varnished."[8] And it can also react with other pigments, like lead white, and even the surfaces on which it is painted, sometimes gnawing through the canvas or parchment of an unwary or unskilled user.

Worse, however, was to come. In 1775 Carl Wilhelm Scheele, a Swedish chemist, created a cheap and versatile new green the color of freshly shelled peas. In a world starved of good green pigments it caused a sensation, appearing in dress fabrics, wallpapers, and artificial flowers, as well as artists' palettes. Charles Dickens was only prevented from decorating his entire house in this one shade thanks to his wife, who took against it. This was fortunate for Dickens, since by the 1870s doctors and scientists began uncovering alarming cases of poisoning involving Scheele's creation. It was proven to contain large quantities of arsenic, which, depending on the conditions in which this green was prepared and kept, could release fatal toxic fumes. It was long believed that one of this pigment's victims was Napoleon Bonaparte, who passed away in 1821 on the damp island of Saint Helena in a room decorated with a Scheele's green wallpaper.

More modern green pigments have been scarcely less troublesome. Pigment Green 7, used in plastics and paper, contains chlorine; so too do Green 36 (used in inks and plastics) and Green 50 (an especially durable pigment used in heat-resistant coatings). All of them make it difficult to recycle green products safely and effectively. And yet green has long since established itself as the color of the environmental movement. We have green power, green homes, greenwashing, green trends, and green politics. Italy, Austria, Germany, Belgium, the United States, Finland, Japan, Indonesia, Senegal, Egypt, France, Australia, and many other countries have "Green" parties. While their policies, priorities, and styles differ, their broad aim is to restore the planet's health and ours, and, perhaps, reimagine the world as the kind of garden idyll that humans have always yearned for. This may not sound controversial—who, after all, could argue against paradise?—but, naturally, things are not so simple. With green, as Kandinsky perhaps divined, they rarely are.

1 Wassily Kandinsky, *Concerning the Spiritual in Art* (Dover Publications, 1977), 38.

2 If anything, the planet is more ocean blue than it is viridescent, as the iconic 1972 "Blue Marble" photograph demonstrated.

3 Algernon Charles Swinburne, "A Match," in *Poems and Ballads* (1866).

4 Johann von Goethe, *Faust, Part 1* (1808) in *Oxford Dictionary of Quotations* (Oxford University Press, 2014), 348.

5 Kandinsky, *Concerning the Spiritual in Art*, 39.

6 I. Bakolis et al., "Urban Mind: Using Smartphone Technologies to Investigate the Impact of Nature on Mental Well-Being in Real Time," *BioScience* 68, no. 2 (2018): 134–45.

7 *The Qur'an*, Verse 9:72.

8 Leonardo Da Vinci, quoted in M. van Eikema Hommes, *Changing Pictures* (Archetype, 2004), 69.

SHANNON MATTERN

Shannon Mattern is a professor of anthropology at The New School in New York City. Her writing and teaching focus on media architectures and infrastructures and spatial epistemologies. She has written books about libraries, maps, the history of urban communication infrastructures, and urban intelligences that exceed "smartness." You can find her work at www.wordsinspace.net.

+ MEDIA STUDIES, CULTURAL STUDIES, ART

GREEN SCREENS
IN EIGHT CHANNELS

Formafantasma, *Cambio* (2020).

Channel 1

We start about 200 feet in the air, then descend through the pine boughs toward the forest floor, where there lies a green screen, an illuminated rectangle waiting to be animated with moving images. The green flips from figure to ground as we watch, as if through a microscope, the subtle movements of blue and green photosynthetic bacteria that incited the Earth's Great Oxygenation roughly two billion years ago. Over the 23 minutes and 21 seconds of Studio Formafantasma's *Cambio* (2020) we cut slices across millions of years of biological and arboreal history – from the evolution of lignin to contemporary forest conservation efforts.[1] Green screens, lying flat on the forest floor or floating upright, sometimes partly obscured by brush or fallen trees, present a succession of images: logging operations, botanic garden collections and Wardian cases, indigenous protesters marching to stake their claim to forest lands, warehouses stuffed with cardboard packaging, CNC machines carving blocks of wood, and landscapes ruined by climate change. Sometimes the green screen retains its verdant hue and serves as a backdrop for burning logs – or as a work surface for hands presenting archival images of logging operations and natural philosophy manuscripts, or hands demonstrating the assembly of a wooden IKEA contraption. Those hands sometimes push *another* screen around the frame, magnifying whatever text or object lies beneath – a green screen amplifier atop a green screen *mise en scène*. At the end of the video, as we climb back up above the treetops, watching the vivid green screen recede as it's framed in by the hunter and forest greens of countless boughs, the narrator issues a warning: "our survival is the survival of trees." We hear the amplified roar of wind rushing through thousands of forested acres, and the screen goes black.

Channel 2

If a forecaster were standing before a weather map, warning us about those gusting winds, we might detect a green halo around their body. Such glitches are the digital artifacts of a cut. Our meteorologist is not actually confronting a map on set; they're engaging instead with a green screen that, on our screens, is "keyed out" and replaced with the map. Chroma key, media scholar Carolyn Kane explains, "is a special effects technique that involves removing color from an image so that another element"—like a map, or a disaster scene, or another galaxy, or, in Formafantasma's case, archival logging footage— can replace it.[2] The background screen's green is "used only to negate itself"; its hue is not meant to be seen by human eyes, but to function as an operative image – a "wavelength and frequency that [can be] isolated and removed so the image can function as an element of another composite." A green screen is about deferral, anticipation, "pending treatment," suspended resolution.[3]

Why green? As Jeff Foster explains in *The Green Screen Handbook*, "the green channel in composite video has the highest luminance value of the three signal colors red, green, and

Georges Méliès, *Dislocation Mystérieuse* (1901).

blue (RGB)...so it gives you more data to work with," and it requires less intense lighting on set.[4] Or, as Lucas Benjamin puts it, "nearly half the photoreceptor pixels of analog video sensors were used to scan for green wavelengths, and so registered green far more precisely. Today, this is still true of digital video chips."[5] But the "green screen" is not always green. Filmmakers have historically used blue screens, and videographers (as well as some contemporary Zoom-casters), green. The key is choosing a color that allows for a clear distinction between figure and ground, so the actors and objects on set stand apart from the backdrop. On the color wheel, blue is opposite yellow-orange, and green is opposite red, which complements blondes and redheads. Furthermore, Kane notes, "because all humans contain about 70% red pigment in their skin, regardless of race, green or blue screen is always better than red."[6] And while green happens to be *my* favorite color and comprises a large proportion of my wardrobe, this is apparently *not* the case in costume design, if the green-screen technical guides are to be believed. A verdant-avoidant wardrobe means we run little risk of having a heroine in a green get-up "keyed out" of her own costume.

Channel 3

But before the blue and green, there was black. Photographers and filmmakers, like Georges Méliès, began experimenting with image compositing in the 19th century. They masked off and repeatedly re-exposed sections of film, or they placed black-clad actors in front of black backdrops or in darkened chambers draped in black velvet, which created illusions of "invisibility, disappearance, or superimposition."[7] Film historian Noam Elcott finds that these "Black Arts," and the broader history of artificial darkness, are "mired in racist rhetoric."[8] Yet the racial dimensions of imaging technology reside not merely in rhetoric and representation; photographic and filmic technical processes were built and calibrated on racist principles, too. As Wendy Chun proposes, race is not simply "an object or representation or portrayal"; it can also be a "technique that one

1 Formafantasma, "Cambio, 23:21," Vimeo (March 2020): https://vimeo.com/394232651.

2 Carolyn L. Kane, *Chromatic Algorithms: Synthetic Color, Computer Art, and Aesthetics After Code* (University of Chicago Press, 2014): 178.

3 Lucas Benjamin, "Colorless Green Ideas," *Bulletins of the Serving Library* 11 (2016): 7.

4 Jeff Foster, *The Green Screen Handbook: Real-World Production Techniques*, 2nd ed. (Focal Press, 2015): 24.

5 Benjamin, "Colorless Green Ideas," 6.

6 Kane, *Chromatic Algorithms*, 179.

7 Benjamin, "Colorless Green Ideas," 4.

8 Noam Elcott, "A Brief History of Artificial Darkness and Race" in Nick Dunn & Tim Edensor (eds), *Rethinking Darkness* (Routledge, 2020): 67.

9 Wendy Hui Kyong Chun, "Introduction: Race and/as Technology; or, How to Do Things to Race," Camera Obscura 70 (2009): 7. See also Ruha Benjamin, *Race After Technology* (Polity, 2019).

10 Genevieve Yue, "The China Girl on the Margins of Film," *October* 153 (Summer 2015): 97, 103, 104. Zoom, the ubiquitous teleconferencing platform, uses portrait segmentation technology to separate users' faces from their real-life environs. But as we've seen in many cases of biased machine-vision technology trained on limited data sets, Zoom has often proved incapable of dealing with darkly hued faces. "I have heard

Chicago Film Society, *Leader Ladies* (2011).

uses, even as one is used by it – a carefully crafted, historically inflected system of tools, mediation, or enframing."[9]

White female faces–"China Girls," "Shirley" cards, and even a particular *Playboy* centerfold from 1972–were central to quality-control processes in photography, film, and digital media. As Genevieve Yue describes, they were "used to calibrate the desired exposure and color balance of film reels as well as the functionality of developing and printing machines." Predictably, "lighting and exposing a film based on a white face often means that the values for everything else–sets, props, costumes, and other actors–are thrown off." Darker complexions are underexposed. Jean-Luc Godard, while on assignment in Mozambique in the 1970s, reportedly refused to shoot on Kodak film because he regarded the stock as inherently "racist." And even though digital technologies make use of a wider range of references and technologies for image adjustment and monitor calibration, the China Girls' influence persists – partly, Yue suggests, because of sentimental attachment. Such engrained conventions "manifest the degree to which white skin is perceived as natural, ideal, and uniquely correlative to instruments valued for their precision and accuracy."[10] And for their position relative to green on the color wheel.

Channel 4

In her 2018 *Typhoon Coming On* installation at the Serpentine Galleries, Sondra Perry juxtaposed various visual elements:

first, a close-up motion graphic of her skin, modulated, magnified, and animated to undulate as if it were a bed of lava; second, footage of police brutality that highlights not the physical violence itself, but its mediation, surveillance, and transcription, rendered on a blue screen; and third, an immersive environment that blends a highly processed iteration of J.W.M. Turner's *Slave Ships (Slavers Throwing Overboard the Dead and Dying, Typhoon Coming On)* (1840) painting with a computer-generated rendering of an ocean. A purple ocean. In Blender, the visual effects software Perry used to produce the work, purple signifies an error – a missing texture. Speaking with curator Hans Ulrich Obrist about the exhibition, Perry explains that she positioned a blue screen opposite the flesh wall "because the blue screen and the chroma key green are supposed to be hues of color that are furthest away from skin tone." Animating much of her work is a question regarding "whose skin tone that was supposed to be."[11] The tones that have historically been "keyed out," those missing chromatic textures, are, of course, blacks and browns.

Perry thus renders her own Black skin larger than life, with a life of its own. "In order to avoid White normativity, I prefer to disassemble my own body. To take my skin, reanimate it into fluid waves."[12] Cultural studies scholar Daniela Agostinho proposes that the adjacency of Perry's skin wall to *TK (Suspicious Glorious Absence)*, the video featuring body cam

Stephanie Syjuco, *The Visible Invisible* (2018).

and news footage, further "juxtaposes the visual history of the brutalization of Black people with the racialized materiality of technologies of seeing," including, as we've seen, China Girls and green screens and surveillance cameras.[13] Some of Perry's other work draws additional chromatic connections between the computer's "blue screen of death," which signals fatal errors, and police officers' "blue wall of silence," an unofficial oath precluding officers from ratting one another out. These resonances suggest that fatal system errors—technical, social, protocological—"are not so much aberrations...as a constitutive necessity of the system," visual studies scholar Soyoung Yoon argues.[14]

The bodies performing this labor—the labor of brutalizing and being brutalized, of policing and being policed, of looking and making things to be looked at—are also central to Perry's work. A "missing texture" in many discussions of labor and exploitation, she proposes, is the Middle Passage, which encompasses the textures of the ocean, and the textures of skin enveloping those bodies "moved *over* oceans in order to become labor sources" [italics mine].[15] Perry re-appropriates colored screens—purples and blues and greens—to create those missing textures, not through evasion or masking, but by imagining recognition as a means to "make a claim instead of being exclusively claimed."[16] "I'm interested in thinking about how blackness shifts, morphs, and embodies technology to combat oppression and surveillance throughout the diaspora," Perry says. "Blackness is agile."[17] In her hands, chroma key is similarly agile. Chroma key, she tells Obrist, is "blackness, it is space, it is sci-fi, it is Mars, it's my grandmother's kitchen table; it's all of these things wrapped into one...The chroma-key, in post-production, it can be anything... The [agility] of blackness exists in the chroma key [and] in this Turner painting, in this ocean," where many enslaved people threw themselves overboard in protest. Perry turns blue screens into oceans so that they might serve as spaces of imagination and liberation. "Given the historical inadequacy of indexical media to document

reports that Black people are fading into their Zoom backgrounds because supposedly the algorithms are not able to detect faces of dark complexions well," Anissa Ramirez told *One Zero*. Some users with out-of-date software and older machines were likewise unable to activate the virtual background feature. The solution? Upgrade your computer! Buy a better camera! And get a green screen. The at-home green screen market exploded amidst COVID-19. Drew Costley, "Zoom's Virtual Background Feature Isn't Built for Black Faces," *OneZero* (October 26, 2020).

11 "Sondra Perry: Typhoon Coming On," Serpentine Galleries, YouTube (May 16, 2018): https://www.youtube.com/watch?v=Qunkb4piXGw.

12 Dean Daderko, "Ill Suns: Arthur Jafa and Sondra Perry," *Mousse Magazine* 57 (2017).

13 Daniela Agostinho, "Chroma Key Dreams: Algorithmic Visibility, Fleshy Images and Scenes of Recognition," *Philosophy of Photography* 9, no. 2 (2018): 145.

14 Soyoung Yoon, "Beware the Light," *Millennium Film Journal* 65 (2017): 33.

15 "Sondra Perry: Typhoon Coming On."

16 Daniela Agostinho & Eric A. Stanley, "Anti-Trans Optics: Recognition, Opacity, and the Image of Force," *The South Asian Quarterly* 116, no. 3 (July 2017): 617.

17 Quoted on "Sondra Perry: Typhoon Coming On," Serpentine Gallery (2018): https://www.serpentinegalleries.org/whats-on/sondra-perry-typhoon-coming-on/.

Felix Burrichter, *Pavillon de l'Esprit Nouveau* (2015).

black life," Agostinho proposes, "digital might be harnessed to craft different worlds."[18]

Channel 5

Filipino-American artist Stephanie Syjuco drapes her green screen on the photographic subject, turning the body into a site of projection. For *The Visible Invisible* (2018), she rendered a collection of historical American garments—a pilgrim dress, a prairie dress, and Revolutionary- and Civil War-era gowns—in vibrant green. Syjuco's choice to work with commercial patterns, which represent more of a simulacrum than an accurate representation of sartorial history, demonstrates how these artifacts help to tailor the "American imagination." By rendering the garments in chroma key, "a color you're not supposed to see," Syjuco calls our attention to unquestioned nationalist narratives: puritan religiosity, Manifest Destiny, and so forth. "It's like manifesting ghosts hauling forward all this American history," she says.[19] Here, those ghosts are embodied as white, blank-faced mannequins, gesturing toward the naturalization of whiteness as a structural foundation for so many techniques of representation.

Her *Dodge and Burn* (Visible Storage) (2019), whose name references a photo-editing technique for lightening or darkening areas of an image, is a riotously polychromatic still-life assemblage of images and objects representing America's colonial expansion in the Philippines in the early 1900s. Victorian garments, tiki torches, artificial plants, and suspended backdrops are rendered in both chroma key green and a gray-and-white checkered pattern that evokes Photoshop's "transparency" background. Set against these "invisible" substrates, both symbolizing their own eventual erasure and replacement, are photo calibration images, color charts, Shirley cards, ethnographic photographs, portraits of Filipino revolutionaries, and stock images of tropical bounty. Here, we see how colored screens can construct an imaginary world—not of liberation, but of colonization, exoticization, and oppression.

Channel 6

Others have deployed chroma key to construct—or critique—new slickly immersive, consumerist fantasy worlds that are the products of colonial pasts (and presents). Felix Burrichter's *Pavillon de l'Esprit Nouveau: A 21st Century Show Home*, staged at the Swiss Institute in 2015, honored the spirit of its namesake: Le Corbusier's 1925 show at the Paris Exposition des Arts Décoratifs. "I tried to figure out what the white boxes of the 21st century would be," Burrichter said, referencing the standard modern exhibition space, "and decided that would be a green screen."[20] The show's chroma-keyed interior projected its guests and furnishings—the work of 30 international artists and designers working with contemporary technologies like 3D printing and carbon fiber construction—into various futuristic settings. While the green surround suggested total immersion, the projections were actually visible only via flat-screen monitors on the walls.

Felicity Hammond, *Remains in Development* (2020).

Still, *ArtNews* suggested that the show delivered a subtle warning: that the "precarious confluence of surveillance and entertainment has radically transformed the sanctity of domestic space," as has been particularly apparent during the pandemic.[21]

Felicity Hammond, meanwhile, critiques the urban growth machine and neoliberal design culture by laying bare the chroma-keyed nature of real-estate marketing billboards and developers' renderings. Her *Remains in Development* exhibition at C/O Berlin (2020–21) is installed in rooms coated in chroma key green, with particular site lines framed through chroma key blue cut-outs.[22] The site itself is just as blatantly "constructed" as the images on display. Hammond's collages mix aspirational utopias and harsh material realities: gleaming towers and rubbish piles. Some images even appear to delaminate, liquidate, and drip down the gallery's green walls. For her "Stone Effect" sculptures, Hammond gathered gravel and rubble from construction sites and melded it with acrylic, coating the building materials in artificial wrappers – just as construction sites are often shrouded with vinyl banners featuring gleaming CGI renderings of buildings-to-come. Hammond frames both the gallery and the development site as green screens. We might wonder what's erased in the substitution. What material precursors and prior inhabitants are "keyed out"? And what generic, placeless developments–plans ready for deployment in any context–are "keyed in"?

Channel 7

Those urban insertions are themselves often green. Inspired by Singaporean Prime Minister Lee Hsien Loong's speech at the August 17, 2014, National Day Rally, where he stood before an unmediated chroma key green screen, Ho Rui An's *Screen Green* (2015) lecture performance examines the semantics and politics of both screening and greening.[23] These annual rally speeches, unlike the more traditional State of the Union addresses in the United States, are typically hyper-mediated affairs,

18 Agostinho, "Chroma Key Dreams," 144.

19 "Stephanie Syjuco: Making Time," *Art21*, YouTube (October 2, 2019): https://www.youtube.com/watch?v=BKFvqKGtjvc&feature=emb_title. See also Sarah Archer, "Stephanie Syjuco: Pattern Recognition," *Renwick Catalog* (November 2018): https://www.sarah-archer.com/writing/2018/12/10/stephanie-syjuco; Jessica Baran, "Openings: Stephanie Syjuco," *Artforum* (November 2019).

20 *Pavillon de l'Esprit Nouveau: A 21st Century Show Home*, Swiss Institute, New York (November 2, 2015). For more green screen artists, see Shannon Mattern, *Twitter* (February 3, 2021): https://twitter.com/shannonmattern/status/1357140367087460352.

21 Stuart Comer, "Best of New York, 2015," *ArtNews* (December 22, 2015).

22 "Felicity Hammond: Remains in Development," C/O Berlin (September 12, 2020–March 14, 2021): https://www.co-berlin.org/en/exhibitions/felicity-hammond.

23 "National Day Rally 2014," Prime Minister's Office, Singapore (August 17, 2014): https://www.youtube.com/watch?v=xEeFZ1ceEVY.

24 See, for instance, Hillary Angelo, *How Green Became Good: Urbanized Nature and the Making of Cities and Citizens* (University of Chicago Press, 2021); Jennifer Light, *The Nature of Cities: Ecological Visions and the American Urban Professions*, 1920–1960 (Johns Hopkins University Press, 2009).

Ho Rui An, *Screen Green* (2015).

with an array of screens featuring renderings that open up a "world of possibility," a "call for investment and speculation" – images akin to the developers' renderings that Hammond works with. Singapore itself is framed as a site of projection; its future is conjured up on the green screen, and those projective images are themselves usually full of greenery. Ho comments on how bountiful botany "seems to sprout out in any futurist imagining of Singapore," and how foliage–real or computer-generated, in the form of potted plants or towering trees–appears in most official media events.

Singapore calls itself the Garden City. Like many other states that have adopted "greening" as part of broader governance and development strategies, Singapore's leaders are continually creating more gardens and encouraging residents to engage in gardening, particularly through state-sponsored community gardening initiatives and centralized community garden districts.[24] Esther Choi writes about how a similarly naturalized urban development model–the "Landform Building" that's sculpted to look like a forest or mountain–benefits from green screen rhetoric: "Landform Building's attempt to assume the appearance of a landscape produces a phenomenon akin to [chroma key's] kind of composite reality, wherein a synthesis of assembled parts is often confused as a 'natural,' seamless hole."[25] In Singapore, many unclaimed green spaces in the city-state, Ho says, are transformed into gardens and branded as "free spaces," which ultimately enables the government to exercise control over their use. Yet just as with the green screen booths one finds in the local shopping malls, where one can pretend to hold up the Marina Bay Sands Hotel or fly through the Gardens by the Bay mega-developments, these community gardens, too, are "fantasy fulfillment machines," promising but failing to "combat the soul-sucking nature of capitalist modernity." Singaporean greenery–both of the botanical and chroma key varieties–*screen* the imagination, "providing a screen for it to be projected" onto, while also "submitting it to a regime of screening, checking its articulations."[26]

Channel 8

One might grow a green screen by coaxing vines up a building façade, using a cable or wire-mesh support system for their growth, or by constructing a system of planter cells. Greenscreen is one aptly named Los Angeles-based company that produces welded trellis systems for green walls.[27] Growing a "vertical garden" on a wall, fence, column, pergola, or arbor– "engineering nature," as the company describes it–has the potential to add shade and sound insulation, mitigate light and air pollution and urban heat island effects, cut air-conditioning costs, aid in stormwater management, extend the lifespan of building materials, provide benevolent security, deter graffiti, and contribute to residents' physical and mental health.

While they do offer environmental benefits, such botanical green screens–much like Singapore's gardens–also have

A botanical green screen at Changi Airport, Singapore.

the potential to serve as smokescreens, as projective surfaces for green-washed, AstroTurfed visions of sustainable urban growth and management. Consider the parking garage clad in trellises and vines or the "vertical forest" concrete high-rise whose balconies are bursting with potted trees. We might also look again to Singapore, where the Changi Airport, seventh busiest in the world, features a four-story indoor forest. "Greenery is unfortunately too often used as an alibi for new developments, by wrapping buildings in green as [the] sole legitimization of an otherwise unsustainable project," landscape architect Céline Baumann argues.[28]

Botanical green screens also often shade their own environmental costs; such projects can be high maintenance and require a lot of water and chemicals to live and function. "Greenery is not per se ecological," Baumann says, "and the commodification of nature can lead in fact to reduced biodiversity and higher pollution." Baumann's proposed solution is that landscape architects be involved in city planning and urban development "in a much more significant way, not just as window dressing" – or, in keeping with our chroma-key theme, as color correctors or special effects technicians. Planners and designers might also engage the complexity of chromatic politics by looking behind and beneath the screen in order to recognize that greenness has both biological and historical roots, and that it requires a vast infrastructural and ideological apparatus to ensure its survival. Within the deep pixels of the chroma-key screen, green is also Black and Brown; it is roiling oceans and outer space; it is erasure and inclusion, exploitation and assimilation, promise and imagination.

25 Esther Choi, "Sustainability's Image Problem," Library Stack (2019): 7. See also Emily Eliza Scott, "Leaky Design for a Broken Planet" in Paola Antonelli & Ala Tannir (eds), *Broken Nature: XXII Triennale di Milano* (La Triennale di Milano, 2019): 50–56.

26 "Screen Green by Ho Rui An," Parasite, Vimeo (2016): https://vimeo.com/140178554; "Screen Green," Ho Rui An: https://horuian.com/screen-green/.

27 See greenscreen: https://greenscreen.com/.

28 Quoted in India Block, "Greenery is Often 'Sole Legitimization' for Unsustainable Buildings Says Céline Baumann," *Dezeen* (October 31, 2019). See also Daniel Barber & Erin Putalik, "Forest, Tower, City: Rethinking the Green Machine Aesthetic," *Harvard Design Magazine* 45 (2018); Yael Stav, "Transfunctional Living Walls – Designing Living Walls for Environmental and Social Benefits," Doctoral Dissertation, Queensland University of Technology, 2016; Sabrina Syed, "Outrage: The False Promises of Floating Gardens," *The Architectural Review* (February 2, 2021). Thanks to Emeline Brulé, Zoya Gul Hasan, Elis Mendoza, Emmet Ó Briain, Rae Root, Alissa Walker, and Tim Waterman for some of these and other references.

TRENDING GREEN
LANDSCAPE IN THE AGE OF DIGITAL REPRODUCTION

PARKER SUTTON

Parker Sutton is an assistant professor of practice in landscape architecture at the Knowlton School of Architecture at the Ohio State University and co-founder of Present Practice.

+ LANDSCAPE ARCHITECTURE, TECHNOLOGY

In his 2011 book, *The Nature of Technology: What It Is and How It Evolves*, author and economist W. Brian Arthur references Martin Heidegger in proclaiming that, "instead of fitting itself to the world, technology seeks to fit the world to itself."[1] In the decade to follow, the fast-evolving relationship between the landscape and social-media platforms—Instagram in particular—would come to exemplify this paradigm. But unlike in architecture, where there is a taut feedback loop connecting digital architectural trends and contemporary studio output, the effect of Instagram on landscape architectural design culture is less evident. Landscape architecture is somewhat unique in this regard, while architecture is less the exception than the rule: many if not most other creative disciplines—fashion, graphic design, advertising—have also experienced accelerated trend cycles driven by an unrelenting demand for new content.

What sets landscape architecture apart? One could argue that, unlike architecture, landscape architecture's digital turn has had more to do with simulation and performance optimization—landscape metrics—than the eye-catching form-making that drives social media algorithms. It could be that landscape architecture Instagram features a larger balance of built work, while much of architecture Instagram is flooded with colorful renderings that, unlike IRL ("in real life") projects, can be produced at a pace and volume that satisfies refresh-happy users. It may simply be that there are vastly more architects than landscape architects in the world, and larger numbers enhance social-media visibility. Whatever the cause, the ease with which one can trace architectural styles and graphic design motifs back to popular social media accounts is greatly diminished in landscape architectural discourse.

In other ways, social media culture has had a very real impact on the landscape, one that may not yet be design-focused but has other, major landscape architectural implications. Consider the viral popularity of the Lake Elsinore, California, superbloom of 2019. After a springtime deluge resulted in an explosion of orange poppies in the Southern California hills, the unparalleled Instagram-worthiness of the landscape drew upwards of 100,000 visitors in a single weekend. Why this crush of people descended on this landscape simultaneously cannot be explained merely by the landscape's unique appeal, however. To properly comprehend this event, it is first necessary to understand the forces that drive content creation.

Among Instagram's defining characteristics is the mass replication and imitation of photographs on its platform. Users go to the same or similar locations and mimic a photograph from their feed, sometimes putting their own spin on it, but more often just putting themselves in it. The Instagram user @insta_repeat [370K followers] offers a rich catalog of four by three spreads of photographs of other Instagram users posting nearly identical photographs of landscape-themed content: the unzipped opening of a tent framing a view of a rocky beach; a person in a canoe with their back to the camera, clad in flannel and sporting a vintage-looking prospector's hat; someone's boot-clad feet dangling over the ledge of a southwestern butte, oxbow river in the distance. Viewed on their own, many of these images appear to show special moments of people exalting in nature's splendor, finding "balance" in a data-saturated world. Taken en masse, they show something else: countless followers living out someone else's experience in a recursive, digitally augmented reality. Stylistically, nearly all of these images and those at the superbloom mark a kind of reversion to the deceptively framed landscape photographs of Ansel Adams, who hid signs of human disturbance from his photographs of the American West. And, in doing so, they elide the critical contributions of subsequent photographers like Lee Friedlander, whose images revealed the extent to which the "untamed" nature presented by Adams was, in fact, set up for human consumption.

Why do users—knowingly or otherwise—create the same content over and over? For insight, one can draw lessons from the market for high-end art. While it may be counter-intuitive, it has been well-documented that recognizability, more than uniqueness, drives demand for works of art.[2] Collectors don't desire a one-of-a-kind piece so much as they want a work that is easily identifiable and, thus, clearly conveys both its worth and the collector's taste. This is the case on Instagram, too, only the volume of self-similar content driven by the ease of replication and distribution pushes the cult of recognizability to the realm of parody.[3]

While trending architectural and landscape architectural sites both draw visitors eager to imitate photos they have seen on social media, the landscape attractions, for obvious reasons, are more likely to be ephemeral. This creates tighter windows for Instagram opportunists, making the waves of visitation larger and more intense. Being landscapes, they are also less able to withstand such crushes of IRL traffic and suffer in ways that architecture does not. In a *Los Angeles Magazine* piece titled, "We Need to Talk About Your Behavior at the Superbloom," journalist Brittany Martin scorned the "hundreds of human beings...clambering about, crushing delicate plants, ruining not just the experience, but the ecosystem."[4] Artist and

author Jenny Odell goes so far as to suggest that we may be headed toward a future where geotagging, the process by which social media users can pinpoint and share their location with other users, "might be seen like littering, a digital action with physical consequences."[5]

Seldom noted amid the excitement over the superbloom's supercharged visual splendors is the grim fact that bloom events like the one at Lake Elsinore are the result of extreme environmental conditions that typify climate change. In this case, an extreme winter drought (which killed off non-native species that compete with the poppies), was followed by intense rain. The extreme climate scenario at Lake Elsinore just happened to create natural beauty, while similar weather in nearby parts of California has resulted in mudslides and wildfires.

Superblooms are not the only climate-change driven phenomena attracting the influencer set. In 2017, the CBC reported major traffic jams in an obscure corner of Newfoundland owing to the presence of icebergs drifting southward from Greenland.[6] The ice floes off this stretch of coastline between Baffin Bay and the Labrador Sea, popularized by Instagram and later dubbed Iceberg Alley, have given rise to a cottage industry of iceberg tours where participants can imbibe cocktails made with 12,000-year-old ice. Together, the Elsinore superbloom and Iceberg Alley are predictive of the potential virality of climate-driven landscape events. What is more, they presage a possible future where today's ecotourism is supplanted by the trending, exotic landscapes of the Anthropocene.

Instagram users seeking virality via the landscape—and there are over 200,000 #superbloom posts—are instrumentalizing the landscape in the service of their personal brand-identity. There is nothing remotely new about this: wealthy patrons have used landscape portraits to convey their bourgeois status and refinement for centuries. For the most popular Instagram influencers, the well-curated landscape and what it symbolizes—wholesomeness, freshness, vitality—is there to sell products that seek to evoke these qualities, such as organic clothes, all-natural cosmetics, even pet food.[7] When this occurs, the Instagram landscape becomes a prop for generating another, unseen green: social media ad-revenue.

There are other, late-emerging ways the landscape interfaces with e-commerce, on Instagram and elsewhere, with equally damaging effects. The flipside of geotagging, which brings people to the landscape, is the internet's commodification of certain plants, which brings the landscape to the people. No plant has been affected by the digital revolution more than the internet's prized favorite: the succulent.[8]

The succulent is perfectly adapted to internet culture in two key ways. First, it is highly photogenic: sculptural, colorful, and available in near-infinite variations. It is, by some measures, the most object-like plant. Second, and perhaps most important, the succulent possesses a number of physical traits that make it unusually well suited to e-commerce: it is highly durable, capable of traveling long distances, and notoriously hard to kill, requiring little water. Unboxed, a succulent is fully formed, uncrimped, and requires little in the way of revival (unlike, say, a fern).

Bygone is the era when home gardeners were limited to ordering seeds through catalogs. You can now purchase a bundle of two dozen Amazon.com succulents for next-day, Prime delivery. Launched in 2018, the "Amazon Plants Store" fundamentally reshaped the online marketplace for succulents by making thousands of plants available with a click.[9] The relationship between succulents' availability on Amazon and their popularity on Instagram is part of the larger ecosystem of consumption and self-presentation. As they possess traits that make them most suitable for e-commerce, succulents are more likely to be bought by millennial shoppers, more likely to appear on feeds, and more likely to trend. This speculation is supported by *Garden Center Magazine*'s annual report, which stated in 2019 that "the houseplant and succulent trade showed up in a big way," representing the fastest-growing sales category.[10]

The graphic iconicity of succulents' shapes makes them readily commodifiable. Since their emergence as the poster plant of the digital epoch, they have regularly appeared on socks, as plastic USB drives, and in cartoon form on various other knick-knacks sold through the web-stores of millennial-driven retailers. In 2017, the Austin-based lifestyle brand Outdoor Voices released their "cactus collection," a line of succulent-themed, desert-

1 W. Brian Arthur, *The Nature of Technology: What It Is and How It Evolves* (Free Press, 2009), 214.

2 Philip Hook, "What Sells Art?" *The Guardian* (November 18, 2013), https://www.theguardian.com/artanddesign/2013/nov/18/what-sells-art.

3 A typical post on the caustic architecture meme account @oh.em.ayy shows a Styrofoam cup labeled "My Portfolio," being filled simultaneously with two flavors at a gas-station soda fountain: "Instagram" and "Pinterest." OH EM AYY (@oh.em.ayy), "I just wanna be featured on @superarchitects," Instagram (January 2, 2019), https://www.instagram.com/p/BsJIReLByhy/.

4 Brittany Martin, "We Need to Talk About Your Behavior at the Superbloom," *Los Angeles Magazine* (March 11, 2019), lamag.com/culturefiles/superbloom-behavior/.

5 Jenny Odell, "The Weirdness Is Coming: A glimpse of the near future as seen through the recent past," *New York Magazine* (November 13, 2019), https://nymag.com/intelligencer/2019/11/2029-predictions-based-on-2019.html.

6 Stephanie Tobin, "Massive iceberg on Newfoundland's Southern Shore attracts shutterbugs," *CBC Radio-Canada* (April 18, 2017), https://www.cbc.ca/news/canada/newfoundland-labrador/ferryland-iceberg-traffic-1.4073428.

7 One example of the countless superbloom Instagram ads shared by influencers: Jordan Orion (@jordanorion), "Someone told me I looked like the part of *Dumb & Dumber* when Jim Carrey walks out in his fringe jacket and now I can't unsee it #fashion [this was taken on the trail if you're about to troll me for the poppies] @pacsun #psgirls #pacpartner," Instagram (March 11, 2019), https://www.instagram.com/p/Bu36rr4BMY6/.

8 For a broad cultural history of cacti and succulents up to and including the present, see: Alyssa Bereznak, "Consider the Cactus: How Succulents Took Over Instagram – and Then the World," *The Ringer* (May 22, 2018), https://www.theringer.com/tech/2018/5/22/17374708/consider-the-cactus-how-succulents-took-over-instagram-and-then-the-world.

9 Emily Price, "Amazon Just Launched a 'Plants Store,'" *Fortune* (February 21, 2018), https://fortune.com/2018/02/21/amazon-plants-store/; Jolene Hansen, "What's Up

hued spandex, representing the hybridization of two 2010s-era mega trends: succulents and athleisure wear.

In many ways, succulents are model plants for the late-capitalist era we live in. Their popularity is consistent with the ongoing and unprecedented urbanization of the US led by millennials.[11] As more people move to cities in search of work and urban amenities like public transit, more gardening is happening in apartments, and more people are turning to succulents and other houseplants. Moreover, millennials, despite being frequently caricatured by older generations for their lack of work ethic, are more likely to be "martyrs" in the workplace according to a 2016 report in the *Harvard Business Review*.[12] This means that they are generationally most likely to "forfeit vacation days," most likely to "make fun of coworkers that take time off," and most likely to "feel shame" about not working. It is no wonder, perhaps, that their generation-defining plant demands minimal care.

It may also be no surprise that millennials' love-affair with succulents has made them a newly significant demographic in the gardening sector. But, unlike previous generations, they "like to grow decorative plants *inside*."[13] Ironically, the presence of plants in millennial homes—plants that subsequently end up on Instagram—may be a direct result of the alienation from nature that many young people feel as a result of modern technology.

The Pantone Color Institute's selection of Greenery, or "15-0343," for its color of the year in 2017, taps into this collective disenchantment.[14] It is telling that Greenery, unlike other recent colors of the year such as Classic Blue or Emerald, is not even a color, exactly. Their explanation reads: "The more submerged people are in modern life, the greater their innate craving to immerse themselves in the physical beauty and inherent unity of the natural world. This shift is reflected by the proliferation of all things expressive of Greenery in daily lives through urban planning, architecture, lifestyle and design choices globally."[15]

Pantone recognizes that plants, even succulents purchased on the internet, are a tonic to internet culture. There may even be a case to be made that the presence of digital plant imagery in feeds has a positive effect on one's well-being. It

with Amazon," *Garden Center* (May 15, 2018), https://www.gardencentermag.com/article/whats-up-with-amazon/.

10 Garden Center Staff, "2019 State of the Industry Report," *Garden Center* (September 13, 2019), https://www.gardencentermag.com/article/2019-state-of-the-industry-report/.

11 Richard Florida, "Young People's Love of Cities Isn't a Passing Fad," *City Lab* (May 28, 2019), https://www.citylab.com/life/2019/05/urban-living-housing-choices-millennials-move-to-research/590347/.

12 Sarah Green Carmichael, "Millennials are Actually Workaholics, According to Research," *Harvard Business Review* (August 17, 2016), https://hbr.org/2016/08/millennials-are-actually-workaholics-according-to-research.

13 George Weigel, "More herbs, More Indoors: Millennials shape gardening trends for 2017," *Penn Live* (December 29, 2016), https://www.pennlive.com/gardening/2016/12/garden_trends_of_2017.html.

14 Nylon first observed the connection between millennial interest in houseplants and Pantone's Color of the Year selection. Taylor Bryant, "Why are Millennials Obsessed with Houseplants?" *Nylon* (March 21, 2017), https://www.nylon.com/articles/millennial-house-plants-obsession.

15 "Pantone Color of the Year 2017 | Greenery," PANTONE (December 9, 2016), https://www.pantone.com/color-intelligence/color-of-the-year/color-of-the-year-2017.

16 Roger Ulrich, "View Through a Window May Influence Recovery from Surgery," *Science* 224, no. 4647 (1984): 224–25.

17 Peterson Khan, Rachel Severson & Jolina Ruckert, "The Human Relation with Nature and Technological Nature," *Current Directions in Psychological Science* 18, no. 1 (2009): 37–42.

18 Mary Callahan, "Plant Smugglers Take 'Massive' Toll on California's Dudleya farinosa Succulent Species," *The Press Democrat* (March 9, 2019), https://www.pressdemocrat.com/news/9327697-181/plant-smugglers-take-massive-toll.

19 Ibid.

20 Ibid.

21 Sandra Garcia, "Poachers Stockpile 'Tiny and Cute' Succulents Worth $600,000, Investigators Say," New York Times (June 3, 2019), https://www.nytimes.com/2019/06/03/us/succulent-smugglers.html.

is now widely known that hospital rooms with views of nature result in quicker recovery times in patients.[16] But, as a 2009 study conducted by scientists at the University of Washington observed, it is also true that rooms with *technological nature* displays (LCD screens featuring nature scenes) result in quicker recovery times as well, even if the effect is dampened.[17] For many social-media users, digital encounters with the landscape are more frequent and, in this sense, more a part of reality than IRL experiences. Might the technological nature on our phones have a similarly palliative effect, accounting for their immense popularity?

Whether Instagram succulents contribute to the health and wellness of millennials remains unknown. Less conjectural is the succulent craze's IRL environmental consequences. Fueled by intense black-market demand, a "Gold Rush-type phenomenon"–or Green Rush, if you permit–has unfolded on California's Central and Northern Coasts.[18] In March 2019, reports emerged from California that "several hundred thousand plants worth tens of millions of dollars" on the black markets of South Korea, China, and Japan had been ripped from coastal bluffs near Mendocino.[19] The succulent that inspired this ecocide is the *Dudleya farinosa*, commonly known as "bluff lettuce." While bluff lettuce can be easily grown in greenhouse environments, the wild-grown plants of the California coast can be 50 to 100 years old, giving them substantially more, and larger, rosettes. "Mature" specimens can reportedly yield up to $1,000.[20] As poaching has grown more intense, surveillance of this vast landscape has increased in turn. In June 2019, the *New York Times* reported on three South Korean nationals detained in possession of "nearly 664 pounds of poached plants estimated to be worth $602,950."[21]

Michael Van Hattem, a senior environmental scientist with California State Fish and Wildlife, remarked that bluff lettuce occupies "a narrow habitat niche in ocean-facing bluffs, above the wave line and below the shrubs, which would shade them out...They need a lot of sun and a particular air moisture content."[22] Further, says Hattem, "their absence contributes to coastal erosion and disrupts the ecosystem, removing a source of nectar for bees and hummingbirds and allowing opportunistic nonnative plant species to get a foot-hold in disturbed soil."[23]

Succulent poaching is made worse by the California Department of Fish and Wildlife's prediction that the plants are unlikely to survive for even a year in East Asian climates.[24]

Not surprisingly, fair-market vendors have also stepped in to meet demand. San Diego's North County has been dubbed the "epicenter of the succulent boom," with "about 45 commercial growers that grow cacti and succulents" in the area in 2015.[25] Altman Plants, headquartered in Vista, California, is the largest of these nurseries. With their purchase of rival Color Spot Nurseries in 2018, they became the largest grower of succulents in the world, a designation that has garnered them national media attention.[26] Their business has recorded such tremendous demand in recent years that it has expanded growing operations to Arizona, Colorado, and Texas, accounting for "somewhere between 7,000,000 and 8,000,000 square feet of greenhouse space for succulents."[27]

Speaking to *Curbed* in 2018, Altman's in-house social-media account manager credited their success, in part, to the careful attention paid to the "internet feedback loop between the plants, growers, and patrons.[28] Altman categorizes its plants into "product lines," which include "Smart Planet" and "Oasis," both of which tout the water-saving and "sustainable" qualities of select plants, reflecting their awareness of the millennial desire to make ecologically defensible choices.[29] The calculus behind commercial succulents' ecological benefits is dubious, however. Yes, individual succulents have low-water needs, but 8,000,000 square feet of succulents do not. One cannot help but question the ethics of diverting water in drought-prone regions to the mass propagation of ornamental plants, let alone the carbon-footprint of shipping them around the country to consumers. What is more, the ever-increasing likelihood that succulents are ending up on people's desks, rather than in their yards, means that the benefit they provide to non-human actors and ecologies is effectively nil.

The rise of the desktop succulent–a plant shared on social media, ordered online, and delivered without ever needing to leave one's home–advances the view of landscape as retail product. Plants become autonomous objects that can be parceled out for our pleasure, rather than members of a complex, interdependent web. This objectification is also an aestheticization, and both the viral landscapes and trending succulents of Instagram aestheticize the landscape, transmuting it into scenery or decor. Both trends are purely visual, and yet they reflect and worsen the typical user's already diminished ability to see the landscape and understand it. While it may seem peripheral to the actual practice of landscape architecture, Instagram's ubiquitous gaze is central to the way a generation of users perceives the landscape and structures their interactions with it. Landscape architecture should familiarize itself with this gaze in the ongoing project of staying modern. Superficial though it may seem, the digital is real.

22 Callahan, "Plant Smugglers Take Massive Toll."

23 Ibid.

24 Garcia, "Poachers Stockpile 'Tiny and Cute' Succulents."

25 Alison St. John, "San Diego's North County is 'Epicenter' of Succulent Boom," *KPBS News* (September 1, 2015), https://www.kpbs.org/news/2015/sep/01/san-diegos-north-county-isepicenter-succulent-expl/.

26 Laura Drotleff, "Greenhouse Grower: Altman Plants Acquires Color Spot Nurseries," *Greenhouse Grower* (January 3, 2019), https://www.greenhousegrower.com/management/altman-plants-acquires-color-spot-nurseries/; Debra Kawahara, "The King of Succulents: Dr. Ken Altman," *Alliant International University Blog* (August 1, 2019), alliant.edu/blog/king-succulents-dr-ken-altman.

27 Chris Beytes, "Capitalizing on the Succulent Craze," *Grower Talks* (November 30, 2016), https://www.growertalks.com/Article/?articleid=22660.

28 Patrick Sisson, "Why Cactuses and Succulents are the Perfect Plants for this Cultural Moment," *Curbed* (April 4, 2018), https://archive.curbed.com/2018/4/4/17199044/cactus-succulents-trend-interior-design-landcaping.

29 Ibid.

IN CONVERSATION WITH
MICHAEL MARDER

Since the publication of Peter Singer's *Animal Liberation* in 1975, animals have been repositioned and reevaluated as sentient beings in both the sciences and the arts. It is only recently, however, that plants are being similarly appraised. Under the rubric of "critical plant studies," philosophers such as Michael Marder are challenging the ways in which plants have been historically (mis)understood and exploited, opening doors to ideas and feelings about our relationship to the world around us that question human identity at the deepest levels. Since plants and our relationships with them are a primary focus for landscape architecture, it would seem important that the discipline be aware of this rapidly emerging literature that seeks to now understand plant life on its own terms. But what are those terms and how can we possibly know them? To explore this conundrum **Richard Weller** spoke to Michael Marder, author of numerous books on the relationship between philosophy and plants including *Plant-Thinking: A Philosophy of Vegetal Life* (2013).

+ Critical plant studies is predicated on the problem of Aristotle's *Scala Naturae*, where plants are ranked below animals, which in turn are ranked beneath human beings. Plants are positioned literally as low life: immobile, mute, and mechanistic. In this regard, the literature of critical plant studies seems to have two interrelated agendas: first, to work through plants to deconstruct this hierarchical philosophy of science; and secondly, as I understand it, to champion plants as subjects not objects, beings not things. As a leading thinker in this area, is this a fair characterization of what is meant by critical plant studies and is this more or less your philosophical project?

Indeed, what you describe is the shape my philosophical project assumed in the first book I wrote about plants, namely *Plant-Thinking* (2013). My goal there was, as you note, two-fold: to unsettle the traditional (philosophical, anthropological, scientific) view of plants as barely living, utterly passive beings, and to reimagine vegetal existence as endowed with its world, temporalities, freedom, and wisdom. Since then, both my philosophy of vegetal life and the field of critical plant studies have grown more ramified, branching out in different directions, and concerned especially with the ethical and political implications of the so-called "plant turn" in the humanities. Still, I would be reluctant to declare the initial part of the project accomplished once and for all. The deconstruction of metaphysics and of the hierarchies it entails is not a demolition derby; it demands lots of patience and a persistent practice. It is not enough to question, for instance, the unfair evaluation of plants as somehow inferior to animals without, at the same time, turning our gazes inwards and interrogating both the psychic and the physiological configurations of *our* vegetality, animality, and humanity. A more positive theoretical gesture of interpreting the existence of plants existentially is, by the same token, an open-ended endeavor, just because this existence cannot be described definitively and objectively within a framework that, as you put it, "champions plants as subjects."

+ Lynn Margulis wrote that the "different wisdom" and evolutionary success of plants lies in their fundamental microbial technologies. In other words, if we are to think like plants we are really trying to think like—or at least imagine the origins of—life itself. Is that the direction of your thinking with plants?

Plants are wonderfully collaborative creatures. They collaborate with each other, with microbes and fungi belowground, with insects and other animals, with the elements, such as the wind that carries their pollen, or the solar blaze from which they draw energy. Of course, they have also developed defense strategies that range from poisonous berries to biochemical deterrents of root growth of other species inhabiting nearby patches of soil. But, before projecting markedly human categories—such as "invasion," "war," or "peace"—onto plants, I insist that we need to consider their unique subjectivity and relation to the world. Plants are not possessive, appropriative subjects bent on conquering more and more territory; if they flourish, spread, proliferate, this is not a conquest, given how blurry the lines separating self from other in vegetal existence are. The same goes for the demarcations between the individual and the collective, which we tend to take for granted in a human world and which we subsequently transpose onto other-than-human existence. What plant scientists call "kin recognition" might be the plants' recognition of related others *as* themselves, while their own organismic assemblages exhibit a very loose integration, capable of separation without irreparable harm inflicted either on the separated members or on the collectivity, from which they are detached. Probing further this line of thinking, we can try to move past some of our most entrenched anthropocentric biases, without, simultaneously, falling into the trap of an abstract and, frankly, undifferentiated thinking of life "as such." That is why in a 2014 paper I proposed the term *phytocentrism* as an alternative to *zoocentrism* and *biocentrism*, alike. My argument, in that paper and related writings, including my 2016 book *Grafts*, is that plants are singular universals, that is, singular living beings who point toward and, to some extent, encapsulate the universality of life. In rhetoric, there is a word for this kind of representation of the whole by its part: synecdoche.

+ Given that the meanings we read into other forms of life always to some extent reflect the anxieties and aspirations of our particular historical moment and cultural context, it makes sense that in the midst of the sixth extinction contemporary thinkers are turning to flora and fauna as philosophical subjects. But as you do this work how do you negotiate the problem of anthropomorphic projection and how do you square that with science and philosophy's commitment to truth?

Although I've already touched upon the problem of anthropomorphic projection in my answer to your previous question, a lot more can be said about it. My goal is not to ascribe human qualities to plants but, on the contrary, to produce an estrangement effect within ourselves by acknowledging the repressed elements of vegetality in us. The persistence of the vegetal principle of vitality–the Aristotelian to *threptikon*– in all forms of life, be they plant, animal, or human, is one path toward such an acknowledgment. Another is the vegetalization of our individual and collective bodies. In this sense, the skin is our most vegetal organ, breathing on the surface through its pores, sensitive to light, temperature shifts, and humidity gradients, "listening" by way of receiving vibrations on its surface. Dry, dead skin flakes and falls off, without causing us much harm. How is it different from a leaf? And our political and technological bodies, too, are vegetal, if you take into account the decentralization of authority, the multipolarity of power, the networked, ramified, or rhizomatic character of human assemblages. Learning from plants will only be possible on the condition that we hold in check the pervasive temptation to project and anthropomorphize. This, in fact, has been a constant of my work with plants: not to obliterate their difference both outside and with ourselves. For, what can we really learn from a shadow image or a mirror reflection of ourselves?

+ Your work, and that of your colleagues in critical plant studies, leads us into a realm of heightened sensitivity to and respect for the lifeforms we have long exploited. In the first instance this is a philosophical project but can you also speak briefly to the practical and political consequences? Surely critical plant studies doesn't envision a return to Eden but, if so, then what is its better world?

When I say that we ought to recognize the consequences of vegetalizing our individual and collective bodies, I have in mind, in the first instance, the practical and political effects of such vegetalization. To take the political sphere, nearly 10 years ago, I wrote a brief analysis of the Occupy Movement, signaling that there has been a shift from the animal-organismic model of political protest to a more vegetal model: participants in Occupy did not march in the streets, but stayed put in a spot, almost rooting themselves in it. The movement then grew and decayed in a decentered way, both locally and globally, flourishing in parts, while at the same time declining in others. However, such vegetal politics is not only the ideal (and, increasingly, the practice) of anti-capitalist resistance. For all the intellectual animosity, widespread on the Left, to sovereignty and centralized authority, these are not today's enemies; we conjure them up, at best, from the day before yesterday. Anarchic plant-inspired resistance to the consolidated organization of an animal-like totality is nothing but an illusion. Without knowing it, establishment politics, too, is vegetal – hylomorphic, mutable, not directly oppositional, modular, anarchically growing, and decaying. The clash is taking place within the folds of vegetality, which is, with the mediation of the image of the network or the web, imperceptibly defining our idea of being as such. That said, plants can, in very concrete ways, point toward a better world. For one, the stifling nature of the collective pressure on individuals is overcome on the terms of vegetal singular multiplicities. For another, our dietary habits may be ethically improved not only if we incorporate more plants into our diets, but also if we learn from plants the meaning of eating with the least violence possible, tapping into the generously self-regenerative character of vegetal existence. Philosophically speaking, these nutritive principles extend beyond the world of plants – most importantly, to lab-grown meat, in which animal cells no longer proliferate as they do in a complete organism. So, to sum up, the political and practical implications of plant-thinking are virtually inexhaustible, but they do not always lead to an ideal situation of "Paradise regained," since the current world of networks and decentered power structures is already vegetal. As it often happens, a radical change has taken place, and the point is to spot it and to draw the right conclusions from it.

+ It seems to me that you are asking us– and helping us–to take extraordinary leaps of imagination and that this is preparing the ground for different ways of being in the world. If so, then in common parlance one might say yours is both a spiritual and an ecological project. How do those two key words sit with you?

I am inclined to welcome these words–spirituality and ecology–provided that they are taken in a very rigorous sense. Concerning spirit, I would say that, for me, it is nothing spiritual, that is, nothing ethereal, purely abstract, elevated. Rather, to put it bluntly and perhaps a little cryptically, spirit is matter's relation to itself. It is for this reason that I am drawn to two German thinkers who seem worlds apart: St. Hildegard of Bingen and G.W.F. Hegel. I have just written a book on each of them, more exactly, on the former's ecological theology and on the latter's conception of energy. And your question makes me realize that these studies, titled *Green Mass* and *Hegel's Energy*, revolve, in different ways, around the brief quasi-definition of spirit I have just given you. Hildegard locates the entire canon of Judeo-Christianity in the materiality of plant existence, as she analogizes the Holy Spirit to a flaming root, Mary to the greenest branch, and Jesus to a radiant flower blossoming on that branch. She also makes the inverse move of situating vegetal life at the core of the creation and continual re-creation of the world. The ecological fold, where the highest spiritual and the lowest material realities meet and where they receive their sense from that encounter, is *viriditas* – Hildegard's signature word, which is the Latin for "greenness" (or, as I've translated it, "the greening green") and which stands, more broadly, for the freshness and the self-refreshing character of existence.

Hegel, in his turn, understands by spirit (*Geist*) the preserving, determining, and elevating self-negation of each thing, initially misrecognized as absolutely other (nature) or readily acknowledged as an outcome of human industry (culture). That is to say, spirit is the self-relationality of matter, and the more intensely matter relates to itself, by negating and elevating itself, the richer, the more determinate it becomes. What fascinated me in Hegel's thought was how his conception of spirit dovetailed with energy, conceived not as a pure potentiality that may be extracted from everything that is, but, on the contrary, as actuality (*Wirklichkeit*) and the process of actualization. My study of Hegel revolves around this dialectical notion of energy. In his *Philosophy of Nature*, Hegel admittedly attributed to plants a nascent subjectivity still largely devoid of self-relationality. This is a serious blunder, given the notion of spirit as matter's relation to itself. But he more than compensated for it when, for instance, he pictured the entire process of the development of spirit on the model of plant germination, growth, blossoming, and decay.

+ *The Chernobyl Herbarium*–an exquisite book that interleaves your writing with rayographs of plants from the exclusion zone by artist Anaïs Tondeur–suggests that you are interested in aesthetics and collaborations with artists. Are you currently working on or planning any artistic collaborations?

Green Mass, the book on St. Hildegard of Bingen I have already mentioned, is actually a collaboration with Swedish celloist and composer Peter Schuback. The title of the book is purposefully ambiguous: in English, "mass" can refer to liturgical Church service or to the sheer weight of things. I like this word for its capacity to gather into itself the most spiritual and the most material connotations in a unique blend we've just discussed. But, from the outset, when I barely started nurturing the idea of the book, it was clear to me that the project would be impoverished without a musical component, not only because it would be robbed of the sonorous connotations of a mass, but also because music and musicality (in a sense that is quite cosmic) were so cherished by Hildegard herself. I was overjoyed with Peter's acceptance of my invitation to collaborate. We discussed the threads of my philosophical engagement with Hildegard, and Peter did an amazing job of composing the score of *Green Mass*,

Linum usitatissimum

Byrsonima lucida

Linum usitatissimum

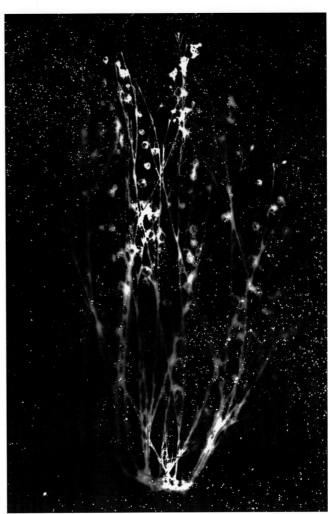

Linum strictum

The Chernobyl Herbarium by Anaïs Tondeur
(2011–2016), 24 x 36 cm pigment prints on
rag paper. These rayographs were created
by the direct imprint of plant specimens from
a radioactive herbarium in the Chernobyl
Exclusion Zone, Ukraine, on photosensitive
plates. Radiation level: 1.7 µSv/h.

which resonated with the themes of my text, on the one hand, and Hildegard's musical heritage, on the other. So, the book's chapters share their titles with the main movements of Peter's compositions, even as his "Composer's Notes" elucidate the relation between textual and musical elements. The publisher, Stanford University Press, will integrate images of the score into the book and will make the link to the musical files available on a dedicated webpage for readers to enjoy this joint effort. In addition, I continue collaborating with Anaïs Tondeur on two projects. One is *The Chernobyl Herbarium*, which turned out to be an ongoing adventure. After its original publication in 2016, we've continued marking each subsequent anniversary of the Chernobyl disaster with a new rayograph and textual fragment. For the 35th anniversary this year, a Spanish edition of the book is being prepared with these additional materials. The other work we have been developing over the past years is an attempt to reinvent the very shape of an artist-philosopher collaboration (the method, if you will) by following plants. Schematically speaking, we strive to adopt a vegetal way of being, or of becoming, and to let it guide our respective practices converging around this common theme. I would go so far as to say that the insistence on collaboration as a fundamental feature of plants in my response to your earlier question and in this brief report about my recent work with artists is not accidental. The collaborative act—assuming that we begin to comprehend all the synergies, modalities of work and play, complicities, complexities of engagement, and so on that it involves—is highly indebted to plants. When I started working *on* them, I quickly realized that this work is only worthwhile if I work *with* them. But this "with-work" (which is the literal translation of Greek-based *synergy* and Latin-inflected *collaboration*) does not impose strict limits on who or what it is that one is working with. Various collaborations with plant scientists, philosophers, and artists are, therefore, of a piece with our collaborations with plants.

+ Speaking of philosopher-artist collaborations, I'm reminded of Jacques Derrida working with the architects Peter Eisenman and Bernard Tschumi on a concept for a garden within the Parc de la Villette in Paris. But not only that, the entire history of gardens is richly imbricated with philosophy. Are you interested in landscape aesthetics and garden design, both historical and contemporary, in relation to plant-thinking?

Definitely. I had a chance to reflect on gardens and philosophy in *The Philosopher's Plant* (2014). A royal garden is the setting for the chapter on Leibniz, in which I also discuss, among other things, the Leibnizian concept of matter as "a garden within a garden within a garden." More recently, I penned an essay for the British online magazine, *The Learned Pig*, titled "The Garden as Form." Precisely as instantiations of a philosophico-architectural form, I find gardens problematic. In their very concept, they entail an enclosure, within which, as I write in that piece, "the most diverse beings are primed for appropriation." Approached uncritically, gardens offer ample opportunities for taming, domesticating, and managing whatever remains of nature. Gardening (and, perhaps, garden design) then becomes indistinguishable from what I call *guardening*, keeping a piece of the vegetal and animal world within clearly enforced, or at least enforceable, limits. Besides the fact that these have been my philosophical engagements with the topic thus far, there is a deeper reason for juxtaposing the Leibnizian view of garden as matter and the idea of garden as form. I think that landscape aesthetics and garden design can strive, in a plethora of ways, to deformalize this form, which we like to impose onto vegetation and onto other kinds of life. Rewilding may be one outcome of such an exercise, but it is by no means the only one. What I find particularly interesting is that the infinity, which Leibniz factors into his notion of matter, makes the task at hand equally infinite. At both extremes of matter and form, we encounter a garden, which means that they are not quite the disarticulated extremes we take them for: matter reaches us replete with its forms, and form is always variously mattered. The deformalization I have in mind, then, does not aim at something like pure matter, but at the infinity of forms that matter gives to itself, for instance, as a garden. The question is: how can the confines of a crude, "imposed" form be relaxed so as to allow gardens within gardens within gardens to flourish? How can gardening persist without being constantly on guard against potential intruders (the unwanted species and shapes of growth), without policing the limits of a plot of land and of our idea as to what this plot should look like?

+ When you were speaking earlier about your collaboration with a musician for *Green Mass*, I wondered what you thought of the recent event where the UceLi Quartet played Puccini's *Chrisantemi* [Chrysanthemums] to an audience of 2,292 plants in Barcelona's Gran Teatre del Liceu, following which the plants were distributed to healthcare workers?

To be honest, I had mixed feelings about this event. The photographs of the Gran Teatre del Liceu were gorgeous, with plants occupying all the seats. Visually, the contrast between gilded balconies and ceilings, the bright red of the carpets and the stage curtains, and the green audience was quite powerful. But I also felt a sense of unease. Plants were put in the role of spectators, uninvolved in what was happening on stage. How is that different from using them as props? In fact, it seemed that the entire theater was converted into a set with 2,292 vegetal elements. The concert was not intended for the plants; it was broadcast online for a human audience. Plants were, once again, used as means, through which organizers wanted to make their point about how the COVID-19 pandemic brought us closer to nature. (I actually think that the pandemic had the opposite effect of exacerbating all kinds of alienation, from the economic to the interpersonal, not sparing our relation to plants and animals, either.) And this is not even to mention that, for the most part, human spectators themselves are reduced to caricaturized plants: passive, separate from the action, silent and immobile until the final applause. So, it was not a big stretch to replace people with plants. For a much more radical and innovative proposal to put plants on stage no longer as mere props and to vegetalize a human actor, I would recommend Manuela Infante's play *Estado Vegetal* ["Vegetative State"].

It's Not Easy Bein' Green

SONJA DÜMPELMANN

Tab: IX.

1 cyaneus
2 coeruleus
3 azureus
4 caesius
5 atrovirens
6 aeruginosus
7 prasinus
8 flavovirens
9 glaucus
10 luteus
11 ochraceus
12 pallide-flavens
13 sulphureus
14 vitellinus
15 ferrugineus
16 brunneus
17 fuscus
18 badius
19 aurantiacus
20 miniatus
21 lateritius
22 coccineus
23 carneus
24 croceus
25 puniceus
26 sanguineus
27 roseus
28 atro-purpureus
29 violaceus
30 lilacinus
31 ater
32 niger
34 griseus
35 canus

Mensura trium unci

lineae sex.

Rezell Fecit

Sonja Dümpelmann is an associate professor at the University of Pennsylvania Weitzman School of Design. She is the author and editor of several books, most recently the award-winning *Seeing Trees: A History of Street Trees in New York City and Berlin* (2019). She has served as President of the Society of Architectural Historians Landscape History Chapter and as Senior Fellow in Garden and Landscape Studies at the Dumbarton Oaks Research Library and Collection, Washington DC.

╋ LANDSCAPE ARCHITECTURE, HISTORY

Previous: Garden color table from Carl Ludwig Willdenow's *Grundriss der Kräuterkunde* (1792). Next: Gertrude Jekyll's planting plan for the green garden in a color garden row.

Joe Raposo's popular song "It's Not Easy Bein' Green," first performed in 1970 by Jim Henson as Kermit the Frog in *The Muppet Show*, is a charming rumination on finding one's identity and place in the world. Kermit first laments his green coloration that "blends in with so many ordinary things," but he then realizes its many qualities and concludes by embracing his greenness. Landscape architecture would do well to follow Kermit's lead by recognizing its green roots in the plant world and by embracing the purported ordinariness of many of its tasks that seemingly ordinary spaces like backyards, roadways, and waste dumps offer it.

Landscape architecture, we can arguably claim, has the potential to be a green profession: an occupation that seeks to create living environments that respect and protect both human and nonhuman nature, as well as its resources. It is also a profession that quite literally works with green plants and that, as some of its first exponents noted in the late 19th century, is inherently interdisciplinary. Landscape architect Charles Eliot explained in 1896 that the new profession was a synthesis of agriculture, horticulture, and forestry, as well as engineering and architecture.[1] Besides working between the disciplines, landscape architecture deals with in-between spaces, that is, with spaces between buildings on scales ranging from window boxes to entire regions. The profession's preoccupation with plants and spaces in-between poses challenges because both are often overlooked. As I have argued elsewhere, landscape architecture has throughout its history suffered various types of "plant blindness."[2] In what follows I will show how this is closely connected to a history of "color blindness," in particular as it pertains to green. Green color blindness in this context implies that green plants, the spaces they form, and the places they create—in other words, the relevant subjects of landscape architecture—are overlooked. Even within landscape architecture green has often been considered a base or backdrop, and as such it has been taken for granted and considered literally and figuratively as "common." Yet, it has also been charged with elitism. Green in landscape architecture has been both essential and expendable. By identifying green's multiple roles in landscape architecture and connecting the green threads in its history with those in the history of science, it becomes apparent how landscape architecture's future strength can be green.

Green Matter(s)

To understand why plant blindness conditions green color blindness, and vice versa, and to understand their effects on the perception of landscape architecture, it is helpful to look at the association of green with vegetation and with the spaces formed by it. Already in Roman times the Latin word for green, *viridis* (sometimes written as *uiridis*) was most commonly used to describe crops and the Italian countryside. Viridis belonged to plants and leaves, denoting both their color and growth. As classics scholar Mark Bradley has explained, "To describe, think of, experience *uiridis* for a Roman was to engage in a conceptual world of cultivation and growing."[3] By the Middle Ages, the adjective green was also used as a noun to denote vegetation and foliage. Similarly, the Anglo-Norman *vert* (which means green in modern French) was used in Britain's early medieval forest laws to designate woody plants and leafy cover in royal forests. Soon this material connotation was complemented by a spatial one. Describing some of the basic principles of what we today would call forests' spatial ecology, 16th-century gamekeeper John Manwood differentiated between the "over vert," meaning tall trees, and the "nether vert," describing shrubs and other low-growing woody plants.[4] Green took on a spatial connotation in other ways as well: near the village or town the common grassy land became the village green, the bleaching-green, and sometimes even the bowling-green. Once the 15th-century modern game of golf had reached popularity, green was also used to designate a golf course, which still today has a putting green. As these cases show, green was often employed as a synonym for grassland, and especially for a grassy place used for social purposes. It was only logical that parks, gardens, and other vegetated areas would be colored green in cartographic representations like city maps and plans. In earlier times, these were hand-colored, but after the invention of lithography in 1796 color also became part of the cartographic printing process. The 1893 metropolitan park system plan for Boston is an early example of a photo-lithographed landscape plan with green indicating existing park areas and brown showing areas still to be transformed.[5]

Green Gap

Although humans have always associated plants with green, not all plants appear green; consider, for example, the copper beech. Chlorophylls, the photosynthetic pigments that cause plants' greenness and that in the case of the copper beech are overlaid by red and blue pigments, were only discovered in the early 19th century. In 1817, pharmacists Pierre Joseph Pelletier and Joseph Bienaimé Caventou called the green substance *chlorophyle*: the color of leaves.[6] Chlorophyll is vital for photosynthesis, and it renders plants green because it absorbs more light from the blue and red spectra than from the green spectrum – a phenomenon called the "green gap." Researchers have recently suggested that the cell walls also play a role in plants' green light reflection.[7] Before the secret of plants' green color became known some scientists had attributed it to light particles, others to the iron found in plants and its reaction with phosphoric acid and air. Others again considered it simply the result of a mixture of yellow plant juices with an inherent blue powder, similar to that of the plants in the Indigofera family. This assumption was countered by the French chemist Claude Louis Berthollet who argued that plants' green color could not be a mix of yellow and blue given that green light was not dispersed by a prism.[8] Despite this proposition, many early theorists did not consider green a primary color, a status they reserved for blue, red, and yellow. Instead, green has often been seen as a color in-between. As an intermediary it is often overlooked, just like the plants and vegetated spaces it registers. It recedes into the background, it soothes.

Plants and their green color have been attributed with similar healthful effects since antiquity. For example, during the first century BCE, Vitruvius pointed out that the open space enclosed by colonnades belonging to the Greek theater "ought to be embellished with green things." He believed that the air these "green things" produced, and that the walking bodies inhaled, benefited physical health in general and especially eyesight.[9] Pliny the Elder repeated this idea in his *Natural History* written during the first century CE asserting that there was no other color more pleasing to the eye than "the green of plants and foliage."[10] If vast vegetated expanses were not available, the Ancients thought that resting the eyes on a green sapphire (smaragd, emerald) could provide relief. These stones were, so to speak, a portable green landscape.[11] Although Vitruvius's and Pliny's assumptions were based upon the Hippocratic humors and photosynthesis was not yet discovered, the Roman writers were already expounding what we now know to be true: plants produce life-sustaining oxygen, and their green color provides relief and healing.[12]

Green Base

Given that life on earth depends on "green things," it is perhaps all the more astounding that plants and the spaces they form are so often overlooked or taken for granted. Yet, even for botanists, horticulturalists, and landscape designers the color green has often played, if not a minor role, then one that forms a base, color datum, or backdrop that is presupposed. For example, German botanist Carl Ludwig Willdenow–whose 1792 book *Grundriss der Kräuterkunde*[13] was one of the first botanic works to thematize plant colors and include a color table–explained that only those plant parts that were of a color other than green were said to be "colored," a terminology embraced by British horticulturalist John Claudius Loudon in his 1822 *Encyclopaedia of Gardening*.[14] The relegation of green as presupposed outlier in the early-modern botanical color spectrum was mirrored by poet and amateur gardener William Mason who stated that gardeners did not need green flowers since plants' leaves were "constantly Green."[15] Mason's contemporary, the politician and writer Thomas Whately, in his famed *Observations on Modern Gardening* (1770), considered green to be plants' "*permanent*" color whereas any red or other color in blossoms, berries, and fall foliage was "an *accidental* colour."[16] The shades of green were, he remarked, most "important on the broad expanse...and by their union, or their contrast" they produced "effects not to be disregarded in scenes of extent and of grandeur."[17] Among other things, the combination of green hues could be used for spatial effect, shortening and lengthening perspectives.[18] On the ground, as well, green reigned supreme. No trickery was too deceitful: green pigments were not only used to color ideal garden visions on paper, but to temporarily render actual barren ground verdant. Loudon advised his contemporary

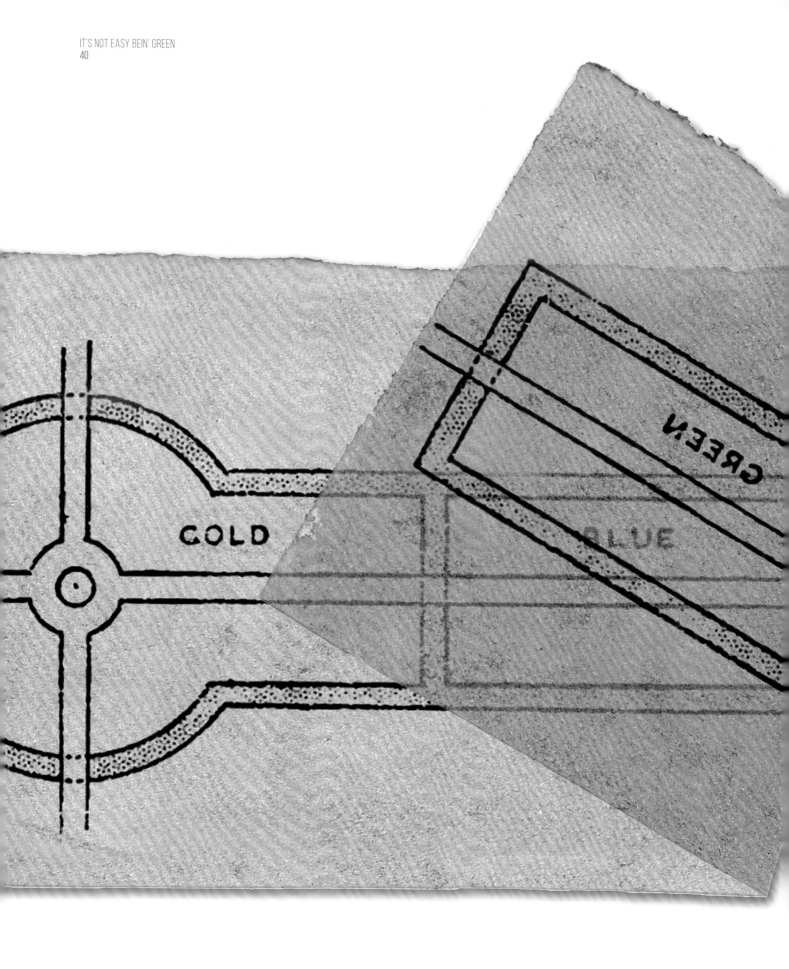

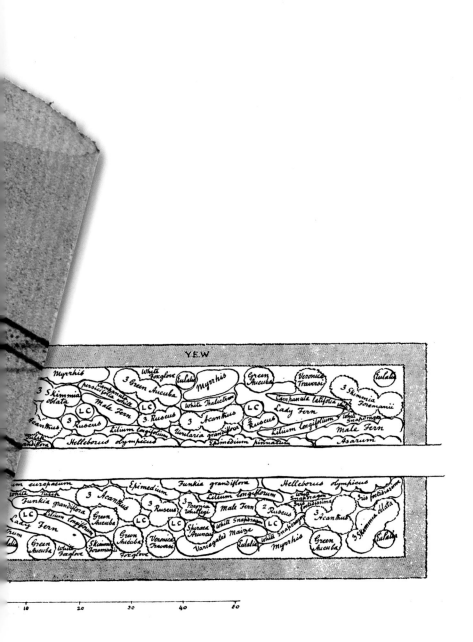

1 Charles Eliot in a letter addressed to Charles Francis Adams, December 12, 1896, in Charles W. Eliot, *Charles Eliot, Landscape Architect* (Houghton Mifflin, 1902), 630–31; Sonja Dümpelmann, "'Landscape Architect better carries the Professional Idea': On the Politics of Words in the Professionalization of Landscape Architecture in the United States," in Joachim Wolschke-Bulmahn & Sabine Albersmeier (eds), *From Garden Art to Landscape Architecture: Traditions, Re-Evaluations, and Future Perspectives* (AVM Edition, 2021), 55–70.

2 Sonja Dümpelmann, "Plants," in Richard Weller (ed.), *The Landscape Project* (ORO Editions, in press). For "plant blindness," see James H. Wandersee & Elisabeth E. Schussler, "Toward a Theory of Plant Blindness," *Plant Science Bulletin* 47, no. 1 (2001): 2–9.

3 Mark Bradley, *Colour and Meaning in Ancient Rome* (Cambridge University Press, 2009), 6–8.

4 All plants bearing fruit also fell under the category "special vert." John Manwood, *Manwood's Treatise of the Forest Laws* (In the Savoy, printed by E. Nutt (executrix of J. Nutt, assignee of E. Sayer) for B. Lintott, 1717 (first circulated privately in 1592)), 26, 359.

5 See Charles Eliot, *A Report upon the Opportunities for Public Open Spaces in the Metropolitan District of Boston, MA, made to the Metropolitan Park Commission*, 1892 (Wright & Potter Printing Co., 1893); Charles Eliot, *Map with overlay showing proposed parkways and open spaces for southern part of metropolitan Boston*, 1895.

6 Joseph Pierre Pelletier & Joseph Bienaimé Caventou, "Notice sur la matière verte des feuilles," *Journal de Pharmacie* 3, no. 11 (1817): 486–91.

7 Olli Virtanen, Emanuella Constantinidou & Esa Tyystjärvi, "Chlorophyll does not reflect green light – how to correct a misconception," *Journal of Biological Education* (2020).

8 Carl Ludwig Willdenow, *Grundriss der Kräuterkunde zu Vorlesungen* (Haude und Spener, 1792), 321.

9 Vitruvius Pollio, *The Ten Books on Architecture*, transl. by Morris Hicky Morgan (Dover Publications, 1960), book V, chapter IX, 155.

10 Pliny, the Elder, H. Rackham, *Natural History: with an English Translation, vol. 10* (Harvard University Press), Book 37, 62, 63.

11 Ibid., 62; also see, Jean Trinquier, "Les vertus magiques et hygiéniques du vert dans l'antiquité," in Laurence Villard (ed.), *Couleurs et vision dans l'antiquité Classique* (Publications de l'université de Rouen, 2002), 97–128.

12 For the attribution of healing capacities to the color green in antiquity, see Trinquier, ibid.; Mark Bradley, *Colour and Meaning in Ancient Rome* (Cambridge University Press, 2009), 7–8; For recent studies on the relationship between green vegetation and human health, see, e.g., Xiangrong Jiang, Linda Larsen & William Sullivan, "Connections

EMERALD GREEN

EQUIVALENT TO

BRITISH COLOUR COUNCIL	Emerald B.C.C. 213
RIDGWAY	Nil
REPERTOIRE	Nil
OSTWALD	

History :

A colour name dating from the 16th century being a general representation of the colour of the gem.

758/3

758/2

Foreign Synonyms :

Dutch :   Smaragdgroen
French :   Vert emeraude
German :   Smaragdgrün
Italian :   Verde Smeraldo
Latin :   Smaragdinus
Spanish :   Verde esmeralda

758/1

Horticultural Examples :

758/3

758/2

758/1

758

758

colleagues employed on wealthy estates: in case "After a dry Summer your Lawn is covered with Brown Blotches...Water these places with lime water, mixed with green colour."[19]

Elitist Green

Color emerged as a hot topic in 19th-century European landscape gardening when many new brightly colored, blossoming plant species were brought to the continent by colonial interests from tropical parts of the world. Lavish plants begged to be lavishly displayed. First cultivated in glass houses, they were then "bedded out" in masses for show. Planted in elaborate symmetrical patterns they filled carpet beds on pleasure grounds. The lawns in front of mansions and country houses provided an ideal green base and background for the colorful displays broadcasting the landowners' elevated status.

But by the 1870s, "greenists" stood against "colourists."[20] As in art and fashion, in landscape gardening bright, strong colors became increasingly associated with vulgarity, the poor, and the purportedly primitive, uncivilized peoples that the British encountered in their colonies and had turned into their slaves and servants. Attacking colorful displays on carpet beds, the greenists paired the idea of green color's neutrality and optical relief with a renewed association of green with elitist space and taste. Green and more naturalistic planting designs regained the upper hand. At the end of the 19th century, a way out of the contentious question whether complementary colors could be considered harmonious or not was to avoid them completely, or to use them in separate, yet related garden spaces. In this way they would be experienced in temporal succession, and not simultaneously in the same space. Monochromatic gardens that used only one color in different hues besides green became popular in the decades framing the turn of the 20th century. If a green garden was included, the entire space took on the mediating role otherwise attributed to the color alone. For example, the "green garden" that was included in Austrian architect Joseph Maria Olbrich's famous color gardens designed for the 1905 General Horticultural Exhibition in Darmstadt, Germany, was meant to provide a "green base" on which "the blue, red, and yellow flowering gardens rest[ed]." Positioned on the highest ground, the garden, made up of linden trees and grass areas creating green horizontal and vertical surfaces, provided a serene relaxing contrast to the lively and sparkling colors in the other gardens. In Olbrich's words, the blue, red, and yellow gardens were "finely polished jewels accommodated on a velvety emerald-colored ground."[21]

Even the myopic British garden designer Gertrude Jekyll–who, like her fellow arts-and-crafts enthusiast Olbrich, paid particular attention to color effects–in her deliberations on "gardens

Between Daily Greenness Exposure and Health Outcomes," *International Journal of Environmental Research and Public Health* 17, no. 11 (2020): 3965; Scott C. Brown, et al., "Health Disparities in the Relationship of Neighborhood Greenness to Mental Health Outcomes in 249,405 U.S. Medicare Beneficiaries," *International Journal of Environmental Research and Public Health* 15, no. 3 (2018): 430.

13 Willdenow, *Kräuterkunde*, 51; *Principles of Botany, and of Vegetable Physiology*, translated from the German of D.C. Willdenow (Edinburgh University Press, 1805), 49.

14 John Claudius Loudon, *Encyclopaedia of Gardening* (Longman, Hurst, Rees, Orme, and Brown, 1822), 132.

15 Stephen Bending, "William Mason's 'An Essay on the arrangement of Flowers in Pleasure-Grounds,'" *Journal of Garden History* 9, no. 4 (1989): 217–20.

16 Thomas Whately, *Observations on Modern Gardening* (T. Payne, 1770), 32.

17 Ibid., 31.

18 Ibid., 35.

19 Loudon, *Encyclopaedia of Gardening*, 1211.

20 D.T. Fish, "Bedding Out," *Gardeners' Chronicle and Agricultural Gazette* (May 3, 1873): 611–12.

21 Joseph M. Olbrich, *Neue Gärten von Olbrich* (Wasmuth, 1905), 4: "In dieser grünen Basis ruhen nun die blau, rot und gelb blühenden Gärten. Gleich feingeschliffenen Juwelen sind sie auf samtenem smaragdfarbigen Grund gefaßt."

22 Gertrude Jekyll, *Colour in the Flower Garden* (Country Life, 1908), 104–5.

23 Ibid., 103.

24 Ibid., 118–19.

25 Ibid.

26 Abraham Gottlob Werner, *Von den äußerlichen Kennzeichen der Foßilien* (Siegfried Lebrecht Crusius, 1774), 113.

27 Richard Waller, "A Catalogue of Simple and Mixt Colours, with a Specimen of Each Colour Prefixt to Its Proper Name," *Philosophical Transactions* 16 (1686): 24–32.

28 Willdenow, *Kräuterkunde*, 237, and color table.

29 Ibid.

30 Werner, *Von den äußerlichen Kennzeichen der Foßilien*, 113.

31 Ibid.

32 Fridericus Gottlob Hayne, *De Coloribus Corporum Naturalium* (J.E. Hitzig, 1814), 10.

33 Pliny, the Elder, H. Rackham, *Natural History: with an English Translation, vol. 10* (Harvard University Press), Book 37, 62–63. Some 17th and 19th-century authors described grass green with the Latin *smaragdinus*, perhaps because mineral color appeared less changeable than grass

of special colouring" gave the "green garden" relatively short shrift despite the large space it occupied in her prototypical plan.[22] Similar to Olbrich's color gardens, Jekyll's "green garden" provided the most serene and relaxing space, to be experienced after all other color gardens. It was positioned at the end of an imagined color garden row. Bright orange and gold gardens were followed respectively by contrasting gray and blue gardens, their colors gaining "brilliancy and purity"[23] in the context of their flashy neighbors. People would reach the green garden after their color perception had been sufficiently activated so that they could both see the various hues of green more clearly and let the previous more exciting color impressions settle. Nevertheless, for Jekyll the green background provided by foliage was also important in and of itself. She warned, for instance, that its shades of green were not to be disrupted by the "bright, harsh green" paint often used to color planting tubs.[24] "A good quiet green...made with black, chrome No. 1 and white lead" would do the job without causing "foliage [to] look dull and ineffective."[25] Trained as an artist and inspired by painter J.M.W. Turner, among others, Jekyll was, of course, aware of every color's importance. Green hues were not to be disregarded even if they first and foremost provided a color datum as vertical backdrops and horizontal grounds.

Grass Green

Both the distinction between, and the achievement of, certain hues of green became very important in the burgeoning turf grass industry in the second half of the 19th century. After all, green did not equal green. Already in the earliest attempts to codify different hues of green, grass had stood at the center. The grass of springtime and the lush summer grass growing near fresh water gave color to "grass green."[26] British Royal Society Fellow Richard Waller used "grass green" in one of the first color tables established to describe "colours of the natural bodies," including plants, in 1686. Besides several other green hues, most of which remained unnamed, Waller distinguished between "grass green" (herbeus) and "leek green" (porraceus).[27] However, in these early days of color-coding, grass and leek green were sometimes used interchangeably. In Willdenow's 1792 color table grass green was also given the Latin descriptor prasinus, which means leek green, thus conflating the two terms.[28] Early modern authors described grass (and leek) green as the "beautiful green,"[29] as the "high,"[30] "proper,"[31] and "pure green"[32] that consisted of equal amounts of blue and yellow and therefore stood at the center of all greens. It was the green that the Ancients had also associated with smaragds (emeralds) that according to Pliny the Elder were the greenest of greens.[33] Thus, 19th-century landscape gardener Gustav Meyer would speak of the aesthetic merits of "smaragd-green lawns" for cultivated garden scenes.[34] Although colors continued to be

differentiated further and to be codified according to various systems throughout the 19th and 20th centuries, grass green remained a common category, even though its definitions and descriptions changed. For example, flower painter Patrick Syme's early 19th-century color nomenclature based upon geologist Abraham Gottlob Werner's 1774 color treatise no longer equated grass and emerald green as Werner had done. Both grass and leek green were now versions of emerald green, and instead of Werner's six hues of green, Syme presented 16.[35] Color confusion was complete by the turn of the 20th century, and botanists, horticulturalists, and some landscape gardeners attributed the situation in part to color blindness.[36] The movement for the establishment of industrial and international color standards came to prominence in the 20th century, producing the British Royal Horticultural Society's color chart (proposed in 1909, first issued in 1939, and still widely used today), and Munsell's 1952 Color Charts for Plant Tissues with a particular focus on green.

Democratic Green

Nineteenth-century urbanization and industrialization with their ensuing health concerns meant that lawns and grass-plats adorning mansions and country houses on both sides of the Atlantic soon were no longer only status symbols of the elite. Grass playgrounds became constituent components of the first public urban parks that opened in Britain in the 1840s. Frederick Law Olmsted, traveling across England in 1850, commented on them repeatedly. In Liverpool's Birkenhead Park he admired the "field of clean, bright, green-sward, closely mown" that had opened for cricket games in 1847. "Beyond this," he reported, "was a large meadow with rich groups of trees, under which... girls and women with children, were playing."[37] The commons outside Chester's old walls also included a cricket ground with a "beautiful green sward...shaven so clean and close."[38] With these examples in mind, Olmsted and Vaux later furnished Central Park with a cricket ground and playground, and with the Green, a large meadow in the park's southwest area originally designated the Parade Ground in response to the competition brief.[39] In the park's early years more and more grasslands were designated as "commons" and opened for play including archery, lacrosse, football, and tennis.[40] They also served as playgrounds for the city's schools.

In colonial America "green" and "common" had been used since the 17th century to describe gathering places near meeting houses and the open, shared, and undeveloped land used for pasture and agriculture.[41] In urban America, these terms were applied to special grassy areas within public parks. However, the use of these green commons would remain contentious. In the eyes of late 19th-century conservative social reformers and park designers, a balance had to be struck between "common" accessible turf areas and those reserved for scenic enjoyment alone.[42] Although the rule to "keep off the grass" was gradually relaxed beginning in the 1880s, Labor Day parades and picnics, as well as political mobilization more generally, would not be allowed on the park commons. Too big was the perceived threat by the labor movement to the governing class and the social status quo. Park promoters brushed off any proposals by declaring "such gatherings... ruinous to the verdure of the pastoral park" and "discordant with the spirit of such a place."[43] Nevertheless, park lawns and meadows from the second half of the 19th century onward have been used by various movements and individuals for political mobilization and free speech. The most well-known example, Speaker's Corner in London's Hyde Park, stands for the right to meet and speak freely. It was formally established through the 1872 Parks Regulation Act in response to earlier violent protests in the park and officially covers a large park area. Here, women campaigned for suffrage and, during the 1908 Women's Sunday, the park's lawns were designated the centripetal force in a choreography leading seven processions coming from different directions in the city to speaking platforms in the park.[44] Voting rights were also the catalyst for the first demonstrations on Berlin's grassy playgrounds, the city's largest open spaces in its first public parks. The Social Democratic Party realized that the neat flat lawns surrounded by tree lines and earthen berms had potential for mass political rallies, and, in spring 1910 it held its demonstrations against the three-class franchise system on them.[45]

Although these venues later also accommodated rallies that would help bring the nation into Nazi party lines, since the 19th century green open spaces have been used for play and protest, often leading to positive change. The importance of the design and provision of these green spaces and the integration of plants in urbanizing areas therefore cannot be overestimated. After all, it is plants' chlorophyll that produces the oxygen we breathe and helps to sequester carbon, it is their evapotranspiration that cools the air and diminishes urban heat island effects, and it is their green fiber that we and other animals depend on for food. Plants' greenness bolsters health, and it has been central to cultural and aesthetic expression. As the quintessential profession using plants to shape open space for survival, cohabitation, and delight, landscape architecture is in an advantageous position to tackle some of the most pressing challenges of our times. Green is therefore not only the essence, but also the future of landscape architecture.

color. See Willdenow, *Kräuterkunde*, 237. Among the Latin terms Willdenow listed for grass green was *smaragdinus*, a descriptor also found in Fridericus Gottlob Hayne, *De Coloribus Corporum Naturalium* (J.E. Hitzig, 1814), 10. In 1894, Italian botanist Pier Andrea Saccardo used *prasinus* and *smaragdinus* as synonymous Latin denominators for leek green, whereas *viridis* was the basic green in his color taxonomy. See P.A. Saccardo, *Chromotaxia seu nomenclatur colorum* (Altera, 1894), 14.

34 Gustav Meyer, *Lehrbuch der schönen Gartenkunst* (Riegels Verlagsbuchhandlung, 1860), 182.

35 Patrick Syme, *Werner's Nomenclature of Colours, 2nd ed.* (William Blackwood, 1821), 34–37.

36 See B. Daydon Jackson, "A Review of the Latin Terms used in Botany to denote Colour," *The Journal of Botany* 37, no. 435 (1899): 97–106; Fish, "Bedding Out," ibid., 612.

37 Frederick Law Olmsted, *Walks and Talks of an American Farmer in England* (G.P. Putnam and Co., 1852), 79.

38 Ibid., 117.

39 Frederick Law Olmsted, "Description of a Plan for the Improvement of the Central Park, 'Greensward,' 1858," in Frederick Law Olmsted, Jr. & Theodora Kimball (eds), *Frederick Law Olmsted Landscape Architect 1822–1903, vol. 2: Central Park* (Knickerbocker, 1928), 223.

40 Roy Rosenzweig, *The Park and the People: A History of Central Park* (Cornell University Press, 1992), 311–15.

41 Elizabeth Kreider-Reid, "Green," and "Common" in Therese O' Malley (ed.), *Keywords in American Landscape Design* (Yale University Press, 2010), 310–11, 202–7.

42 Olmsted, "Applications for Appropriation of Park Ground," in *Frederick Law Olmsted Landscape Architect*, ibid, 424–25; Olmsted, "Difficulties of Preserving Green Turf," ibid., 428–32; Rosenzweig, *The Park and the People*.

43 Charles Sprague Sargent, "The Use of City Parks," *Garden and Forest* (July 29, 1891): 349. Also see Sargent, "The Proper Use of Public Parks," *Garden and Forest* (September 25, 1890): 457–58 (457); Sargent, "Keep off the Grass," *Garden and Forest* (July 25, 1894): 291; and Rosenzweig, *The Park and the People*.

44 "Women's Sunday: The Great March to Hyde Park," *Votes for Women*, no. 15 (June 18, 1908): 243–46.

45 Sonja Dümpelmann, "Grünes Gras und frische Luft im Hippodrom. Zur Berliner Spiel- und Sportbewegung im Deutschen Kaiserreich," *Neue Landschaft*, no. 3 (2021): 23–30.

VIRIDIC DISTURBANCE

REPROGRAMMING THE TOOLS OF LANDSCAPE MAINTENANCE

Michael Geffel is a landscape architect and visiting professor at the University of Oregon, where he is program manager of the Overlook Field School. His design research focuses on using field exploration and experimentation to understand the generative capacity of maintenance in the construction of novel ecosystems. Geffel's maintenance experiments have been featured in *Landscape Architecture Magazine*, *Places Journal*, and the Ambiguous Territory Symposium.

Brian Osborn is an associate professor of architecture and environmental design at California Polytechnic State University in San Luis Obispo. His research and creative work investigate the agency of digital design and production methods in the coupling of constructed form and biological systems. His contributions to the forming field of digital techniques in landscape architecture have been featured in collections such as *Codify*, *Representing Landscape*, and *Landscape Architecture and Digital Technologies*.

Julian Raxworthy is an associate professor and discipline leader of landscape architecture at the University of Canberra. He holds a doctorate from the University of Queensland and has taught in Australia, the United States, Europe, and South Africa. His most recent book is *Overgrown: Practices between Landscape Architecture and Gardening* (MIT Press, 2018), which was supported by a grant from the Graham Foundation for Advanced Studies in the Fine Arts.

✚ LANDSCAPE ARCHITECTURE, ECOLOGY

Green is a catch-all word for anything environmental, its common usage arising from a recognition that any idea we have about "environment" is related to plants and their basic color – the color of photosynthesis. The Latin word for green– *virent*–gives us *viridarium* (garden), *virentia* (vegetation), and *viridesco* (growth).[1] It is at the root of Julian Raxworthy's proposed new language of plants, termed "the viridic," which he, in his book *Overgrown: Practices between Landscape Architecture and Gardening*, offers as a landscape architectural equivalent to "the tectonic" in architecture.[2] While landscape architectural languages are derived from architecture's descriptions of static form, plants are dynamic, so *growth* is the material itself. To optimize emergent conditions of growth in landscape design, Raxworthy argues that landscape architects must practice differently, operating in real time like the gardener in the garden does, a paradigmatically different mode of practice for landscape architecture.

Viridic Disturbance

Viridic disturbance combines the idea of growth as an emergent condition of maintenance activity with correlates in ecological succession where maintenance simulates natural disturbance to initiate growth, an approach quite different to normal planting design practice. In landscape architecture, planting design is traditionally oriented around a single initial installation of plants; however, this approach is fraught because it requires plants that have grown under one environmental condition in the nursery to adjust to another to survive, with intense requirements during establishment such as irrigation and fertilization.[3] The dominant paradigm of design– predictive speculation with little opportunity to engage after installation–prevents landscape architects from responding to any successive growth since this stage (maintenance) is typically overseen by others. The difficulty of attaining the degree of desired performance through mass planting provided the impetus for us to theorize different approaches to "greening" that prioritize both initiation and care of existing emergent vegetation, rather than planting, while maintaining some of the qualities present in planting designs. Recognizing that landscape maintenance is already the principal mediator of emerging ecosystems, maintenance actions can be reconsidered to accomplish plant-based environmental goals, such as reforestation, at a larger scale than is possible through planting alone. For viridic disturbance, maintenance *is* the planting design strategy, with plants arising from the site's inherent botanical reservoir, rather than maintenance being applied to installed plants, similar to ecological restoration and silviculture, but with an eye toward the kind of aesthetic outcomes that characterize planting designs rather than on restoring ecosystems, to their precolonial state. Such an approach capitalizes on latent material within a site's biological reservoir, which is already attuned to local conditions and therefore reaches desired planting effects more quickly and with a greater rate of success.

What distinguishes this approach from traditional understandings of gardening, or even ecological restoration, is our emphasis on the predictive modeling of plant

 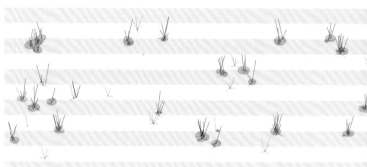

architecture, based on the plant functional type of specific species within that reservoir, and the reintegration of sensed conditions arising from those actions into the model. To accommodate this requires the adoption of the logics of plant growth into the medium of landscape design – the drawing. This is done through what Brian Osborn refers to as "live drawing" – the modeling of plant functional type as a parametric response to maintenance actions such that they can feed back recursively into design in real time.

Maintenance Effects

Landscape maintenance is commonly misconceived as the activity of suppressing landscape change, implied in the word "maintain," which the *Oxford English Dictionary* defines as "to continue, keep up, preserve." However, the essence of maintenance is care, not control, a concept that has been explored in art by Mierle Laderman Ukeles,[4] in philosophy by Robert M. Pirsig,[5] in critiques of landscape preservation by Robert Cook,[6] and at the nexus of social science and landscape by Joan Nassauer.[7] Care is a practice that must always adapt to the changing landscape if a landscape is to "continue" within a non-equilibrium paradigm, since maintenance practices always adapt and evolve based on growth, or how a landscape fails when it is not maintained properly. For example, when maintaining a young riparian tree planting in the maritime Pacific Northwest, the goal is not to hold on to the original form of the saplings, but to foster the saplings' growth process so that the planting eventually produces the ecological benefits of a mature forest. With such change in plant form comes changes in maintenance requirements: early suppression of cool-season grasses and Himalayan blackberry (*Rubus armeniacus*) that may compete with newly planted trees eventually gives way to thinning and selective removal of those same trees as the forest matures. The funding limitations on such a capital project presents an opportunity for our viridic disturbance approach in which the planting plan is decentered in favor of the maintenance manual—or live drawing as proposed in this paper—to care for the volunteer saplings emerging on site to produce a novel forest. These species may be unexpected given the historic ecosystem—for example, black locust trees (*Robinia pseudoacacia*)—but are undoubtedly well adapted to the specific soil composition and climatic conditions of the site.

In ecological terms, maintenance practices can be understood as a type of disturbance event, and correspondingly viridic disturbance mirrors the ecological term "nudation," the "initiation of a new plant succession by a major environmental disturbance," to describe the generative capacity of maintenance.[8] Maintenance catalyzes disturbance responses in plants and ecosystems through events such as mowing, hedging, thinning, and coppicing. By imitating nudation, and initiating succession, maintenance events produce immediate ecological effects (what we call "first-order effects"), and over time these actions produce material, spatial, and aesthetic qualities (or "second-order effects"). We characterize first-order effects as, for example, successful competition of particular species or plant functional types, or the start of certain succession responses (each of which are ecological understandings), and second-order effects as a landscape architectural reading of those same effects, which moves the ecological result into the space of design consideration, and specifically that of planting design.

In Michael Geffel's mown strips—an experimental landscape in a field at the University of Oregon where mowing and cutting is systematically undertaken to elicit plants' responses—the first-order effects from mowing vary depending on the ecological response of each plant. Cool-season grasses compose most of the field and respond to cutting with increased lateral stolon growth (as is the case with a common lawn). On the other hand, the effect of mowing on blackberry removes all vertical growth and encourages prostrate cane development. The effect on black locust trees is very different. When young saplings are mown (which occurs when they are growing amidst blackberry), new sprouts grow vertically from dormant buds on the cut stump like a coppice cut. Cumulatively, this approach encourages the development of tree thickets while suppressing the development of blackberry thickets.

Arising from these same actions, these ecological effects contrast with the undisturbed growth occurring in the unmown rows where plants are free to flower and reseed. These remaining drifts produce a bold graphic, balancing the tension between care and biodiversity, and foster a forest space, comprising the second-order effects that these actions

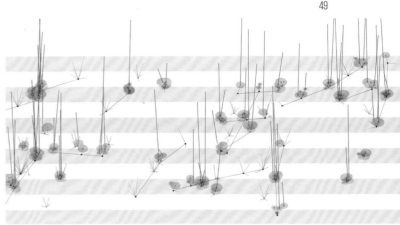

produce, in terms of design qualities, at particular times. Second-order effects are revealed over the growing season. In early spring, last year's drifts are still visible as wheaten white lines against emerald turf, punctuated by the silver stalks of fennel, the black seedpods of Queen Anne's lace, and the gaudy pink of vetch. Over the course of the season, new growth quickly swallows these marks amidst a sea of greens and the pattern is now only visible from above.

While these effects are impossible to predict exactly, they nonetheless exhibit trends and trajectories within more broad levels of tolerance than are expected from strictly designed landscapes.[9] With this knowledge it is possible to reverse-engineer maintenance events to cultivate desirable types of nudation that suit planting design ambitions. Like all trades, maintenance "rules of thumb" are typically used to respond to emergent uncertainty or change in landscapes, bringing them under control on the basis of certain preconceived "acceptable" forms of the landscape, on the basis of the tradesperson's learning from experience. This can make maintenance actions seem either arbitrary or willfully disrespectful to the ideals of landscape architects' designs, making maintenance design even more elusive to landscape architects, since they typically communicate through predictive drawings at a distance.

Operations

Maintenance responses to emergent conditions—and the subsequent effects of maintenance on landscape processes—are inherently parametric, and the shift to parametric thinking that has developed in landscape architecture since the ability to create custom algorithms within computer design software has become more accessible. The field at the University of Oregon is rationalized into alternating bands of mown and unmown vegetation based on the width of the mower deck as a design parameter. Geffel's strips produce "orderly frames"[10] for the operator to then survey and mow when any target species are identified. Timing, or when to mow, is also a parameter that is part of maintenance trades and the interval of the operator. The first round of parametric mowing begins in late spring to "knock-back" the first flush of cane development and produces an abrupt change in the color palette and spatiality of the field. Vibrant green drifts frame views across the site and human

movement is guided across a freshly cut, pale-gold surface. This experience is short lived as a second flush of new growth quickly emerges in the mown areas. The second (and final) mowing occurs in early summer, just as drought begins in the maritime Pacific Northwest. Following this cut, the species diversity within unmown drifts becomes most visible through the flowering of the perennial peavine, fennel, Queen Anne's lace, and salsify. By the end of the growing season the drifts fade to a wheaten white and the mown surface greens again with the first fall rains, interlaced with the coarse hunter leaves of the trailing blackberry canes.

Scheduling the mowing based on blackberry cane emergence suppresses the target species using as little labor as possible. The unfortunate effect of this timing is that the previous year's pattern is almost completely swallowed by an earlier flush of spring grasses making it impossible to follow the same angle. Instead, the angle was intentionally skewed to create a matrix of maintenance regimes. Each unmown drift is thus composed of a grid of two alternating conditions: unmown for two years in a row, or unmown this year but mown last. While imperceptible at ground level, the field moiré is visible from above due to the persistence of last year's seed pods on cool-season grasses that were not mown either year.

This maintenance process is similar to what Osborn has referred to as a process of *extended fabrication*,[11] wherein landscape form is allowed to emerge through iteratively staged and computer numerically controlled (CNC) developments that coordinate multiple material and maintenance processes. Here, the fabrication process, analogous to CNC routing, involves GPS-guided machinery and real-time sensing of agricultural operations, and of course, contemporary vacuum technology. Small-scale, robotic lawnmowers have already arrived with the Husqvarna Automower, which has recently entered the commercial market. Equipped with auto-stop and motion sensors, a pin-code, alarm, and GPS tracking, the Automower has a working area capacity of up to 1.25 acres and can operate around the clock. Like the Roomba, the Automower does not follow a prescribed mowing pattern, but a future where autonomous mowers are programmed to pattern our vacant landscapes may not be that far away. Already, advancements

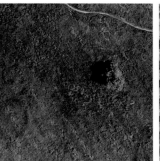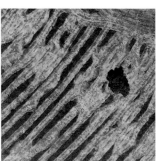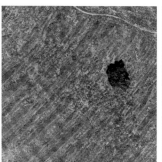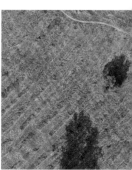

in sensing allow the irrigation contractor to monitor and control an irrigation system from the comfort of their office. With additional sensors to detect undesirable species by their infrared reflectance (a technology currently used in agriculture to target weeds for herbicide application), we could imagine a day when the infrastructural service of maintenance mowing also allows for the autonomous regeneration of landscapes. In this speculative scenario, the landscape architect has even greater opportunity to design through maintenance, but for these designs to be truly site specific the field must also develop new methods of modeling the cause and effect in landscape.

In our viridic disturbance research we are developing algorithms in Grasshopper that allow designers to explore the formal and spatial implications of maintenance operations, represent novel operational definitions, and identify the critical parameters that must be communicated to the maintenance contractor to achieve desired first- and second-order effects. While the simulation will always fall short of modeling the actual effects of nudation, by understanding the trajectory of outcome from certain operations and modeling it, this can be input into actions the results of which can, in turn, be input back into the same model, in a recursive manner. This is what Osborn calls a live drawing, and it forms an important part of viridic disturbance to bridge the space between design and maintenance practices, described below.

Live Drawing

Operating in real time requires a disciplinary shift toward surveillance practices.[12] Typically, landscape design begins with a survey that examines and maps the land's existing features. While working to describe the ground and the location of elements on it, the survey also provides a registration against which proposed interventions are understood. However, surveys are rarely performed more than once during the course of a project and provide a fixed image of site conditions. As a result, important temporal and dynamic processes responsible for shaping the site, such as the effects of maintenance, remain invisible, misunderstood, and under-engaged. Any design engagement with nudation requires an alternative approach – from the practice of surveying toward a practice of surveillance, which, in contrast, implies the ongoing act of *keeping watch*.

It includes the serial recording of data through the use of an expanding menu of environmental sensors, as well as through the incorporation of successive drone-based point cloud data, documenting change. To make this transition from surveying to surveillance practices, Geffel has been successively using a drone to capture state changes over an extended period of time. Utilizing a range of intervals to capture seasonal growth, and before-and-after mowing, Geffel is able to not just map changes in vegetation, but also interpolate what particular types of vegetation look like in his characteristic mappings. While Ian Weir has successfully used surveying information to produce point clouds to represent vegetation change,[13] Geffel has been utilizing software that converts photographs into a continuous surface, representing vegetation as a solid, which has then been contoured as the basis of his mappings.

A key contradiction of the viridic is that it is a real time, non-representational practice; however, representation is inherently tied to design, the Latin root of the word design referring directly to drawing. Consequently, as an alternative to simulation, Osborn's live drawing has the capacity to input information collected by drones and other devices directly into modeling environments like Rhinoceros and Grasshopper, so that digital geometries may be parametrically driven by a continuous feed of contextual data.[14] In a test for this project, Osborn developed an algorithm in Grasshopper that predicted the proliferation of black locust suckers shooting from roots after being mowed, learning from Geffel's successive observations. From this modeling, it is demonstrated that a mown strip can cause a sucker to travel further, and then–if it emerges in an unmown strip–to grow to become a tree. In this way a linear forest can be encouraged by the use of mowing, after which time the operations change and then pruning and arboriculture practices are used to move it to the next stage. If the next information from the drone survey is then inputted to tweak the algorithm, a recursive loop could be created that analyzes and models sensed data about growth, feeding it back into guidance for the operator: the next stage of the project.

Conclusion

Viridic disturbance takes the idea of the viridic to its logical conclusion: by shifting the focus of vegetation management

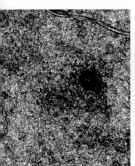 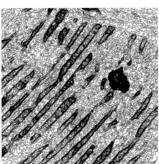 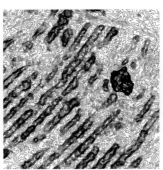 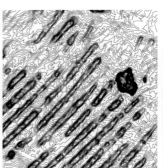 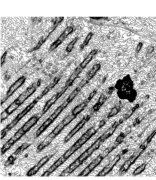

away from the drawing and moving it to the field, techniques that were previously used to maintain the designer's hopeful vision can now care for the latent ecological characteristics of the site. The addition of Osborn's live drawing to the project minimizes the previous binary of office versus field, allowing for a level of engaged design consideration in what was otherwise seen by Raxworthy as a kind of improvisation. While Geffel's familiarity and engagement with maintenance was achieved by working with the operator on site, closing the loop between parametric maintenance and live drawing allows landscape architects to anticipate what the operator's actions will next generate: learning. It's said that "you can't fake experience," and in this project we are aiming to capture the trial-and-error process and extend it slightly into the arrow of time, engaging the almost-living medium of the digital model with its analog, the real world.

1 Michel Pastoureau, *Green: The History of a Color* (Princeton University Press, 2014).

2 Julian Raxworthy, *Overgrown: Practices between Landscape Architecture and Gardening* (MIT Press, 2018).

3 Sami Kent, "Most of 11m Trees Planted in Turkish Project 'May Be Dead,'" *The Guardian* (January 30, 2020).

4 Patricia C. Phillips (ed.), *Mierle Laderman Ukeles: Maintenance Art* (Prestel, 2016).

5 Robert Pirsig, *Zen and the Art of Motorcycle Maintenance: An Inquiry into Values* (Morrow, 1974).

6 Robert E. Cook, "Is Landscape Preservation an Oxymoron?," *The George Wright Forum* 13, no. 1 (1996): 42–53.

7 Joan Iverson Nassauer, "The Aesthetics of Horticulture: Neatness as a Form of Care," *HortScience* 23 (1988): 973–77.

8 "Nudation," in Michael Allaby, *A Dictionary of Ecology* (Oxford University Press, 2010).

9 Julian Raxworthy, "Novelty in the Entropic Landscape: Landscape Architecture, Gardening and Change" (PhD Thesis, University of Queensland, 2013).

10 Joan Iverson Nassauer, "Messy Ecosystems, Orderly Frames," *Landscape Journal* 14 (1995): 161–70.

11 Brian Osborn, "Coding Behavior: The Agency of Material in Landscape Architecture," in Bradley Cantrell & Adam Mekies (eds), *Codify: Parametric and Computational Design in Landscape Architecture* (Routledge, 2018), 188.

12 Brian Osborn, "Surveillance Practices: Drawing the Nature of Sites," in Nadia Amoroso (ed.), *Representing Landscapes: Hybrid* (Routledge, 2016), 220–23.

13 Ian Weir, "Enacted Cartography: Testing a Methodology for Making Site-Specific Architecture," *in Contexts of Architecture* (The 38th International Conference of Architectural Science Association, Launceston, 2004).

14 Osborn, "Coding Behavior."

Previous: Live drawing of the staged cultivation of *Robinia pseudoacacia*.

Above: The contour signature of emergence over the growing season.

TOD GOD

GREENSPACE
ORIENTED
DEVELOPMENT

JULIAN BOLLETER, CRISTINA RAMALHO + ROBERT FREESTONE

Julian Bolleter is codirector of the Australian Urban Design Research Centre at the University of Western Australia, where his role includes conducting research projects for the Australian Research Council and Western Australian government. Bolleter's work focuses on the nexus between endemic landscapes, open space systems, and urban development. His books include *Made in Australia: The Future of Australian Cities* (2013, with Richard Weller) and *Greenspace-Oriented Development: Reconciling Urban Density and Nature in Suburban Cities* (2019, with Cristina Ramalho).

Cristina Ramalho is a research fellow in urban ecology at The University of Western Australia. Her work focuses on how we can better plan, design, and manage urban environments in order to make them more livable and biodiverse. She is interested in evidence-oriented urban greening, conservation of urban biodiversity, and integration of traditional knowledge in urban land-use and water planning and natural resource management.

Robert Freestone is professor of planning in the School of Built Environment at the University of New South Wales, Australia. His research targets contemporary and historical aspects of urban structure and change. His books include *Iconic Planned Communities and the Challenge of Change* (2019), *The Planning Imagination* (2014), *Urban Nation: Australia's Planning Heritage* (2010), and *Model Communities* (1989).

+ URBAN DESIGN, PLANNING

Various landscape and urban design theories have sought to reconcile urban form and green systems in recent decades. For example, Green Urbanism proposes a "city that maximizes landscapes, gardens, biodiversity, and green infrastructure."[1] In a similar vein, Landscape Urbanism foregrounds landscape as the "ultimate system to which all goes, and from which all comes, a template for urbanism."[2] Likewise, Ecological Urbanism proposes an apparently "new sensibility - one that has the capacity to incorporate and accommodate the inherent conflicts between ecology and urbanism."[3] Finally, Biodiversity Sensitive Urban Design provides a protocol for urban design that aims to create a net benefit to native species and ecosystems by providing essential habitat and food resources.[4]

Alongside these sits a mix of planning theories challenging the hegemony of low-density suburban development. So-called "Smart Growth" brings together a broad agenda of development desiderata: planning, natural resource preservation, transportation, housing, community development, and economic development.[5] The compact city emphasizes "intensification of development and activities, creates limits to urban growth, encourages land use and social mixes, and focuses on the importance of public transportation and the quality of urban design."[6] Aspirations for the sustainable city interconnect all these models, notwithstanding the various emphases and nuances brought to bear. The recurring spatial planning strategy that most notably integrates these goals focusing on increasing urban density and enhancing public transport connectivity is transit-oriented development (TOD).

Peter Calthorpe helped codify TOD in the late 1980s, and it quickly became a central tenet of modern planning with the publication of his book *The New American Metropolis*.[7] TOD has varied definitions but essentially aims to concentrate urban activity in high-intensity mixed-use precincts centered on highly accessible transport nodes to increase public transport use and promote urban infill. Delivering urban infill along with greater densification in greenfield development is a *sine qua non* in Australian urban policies across all levels of government. Since the 1980s, urban consolidation has become firmly established as orthodoxy in Australian spatial planning theory and practice, although the results have been diffuse and contested. The former is reflected in the continued overwhelming dominance of suburbia as the major housing frontier. The latter is echoed in community resistance to the proclivity of Australian planning systems in facilitating higher density as the preferred urban form. A significant concern that has emerged for densifying cities, especially in city centers and inner suburbs, is the under-provision of open space.[8] While in more capacious outer suburbs, ongoing concerns are raised by the differential quality of open spaces often correlated with critical social parameters such as socio-economic status[9] and over-dedication to occasional organized sporting use. This is the main setting for our exposition of an alternative model of development weighted to securing a high-quality public realm.

Opposite: Greenspace-oriented development correlates urban densification with upgraded parks.

In this essay we advance the idea of greenspace-oriented development (GOD), which prioritizes sustainable suburban renewal around open spaces.[10] The paper has three core sections. First, we scope TOD's goals, benefits, and experience. Next, we outline a case for orientating development around suburban parks and other green spaces, which are often under-utilized as recreation and leisure spaces when of inferior quality.[11] Third, we outline a practical step-wise method for delivering greenspace-oriented development. Our conclusion reflects on the broader implications and significance of the pragmatic approach proposed. The main arena for our investigation is the middle-ring suburbs of Australian cities developed unimaginatively as speculative development in the post-war era.[12]

The TOD Approach

TOD proponents believe that compact urban form co-located with public transport nodes—often referred to in planning policies as "activity centers"—is a viable antidote to sprawl, delivering densification and many other benefits. These include making public transportation more economically viable, boosting local services, reducing automobile dependency, and helping achieve lower energy consumption and greenhouse gas emissions. Advocates believe it will provide residents with a diversity of local jobs and encourage economic growth, contributing to a higher quality of life for residents.[13] As an achievable demonstration of the critical nexus between land use and transport planning, the concept had near-universal appeal, and "now almost every metropolitan region with major public transport infrastructure has adopted some form of high-density TOD scenario."[14] Indeed, all Australian state and territory capital cities plan to achieve urban densification around public transport nodes as part of their infill agendas. Through such development, these plans attempt to avoid Australian cities sprawling in what is recognized as an unhealthy, socio-economically stratified, unsustainable, and unproductive manner.[15]

The reality of urban development in Australian cities, however, contrasts starkly with the theoretical TOD vision.[16] As Jago Dodson has observed, "despite more than two decades of densification policy across Australia's major cities, there are vast suburban regions of low-density development."[17] Indeed, Australian cities still have some of the lowest population densities globally – Melbourne, Adelaide, Perth, and Brisbane, averaging only 16, 14, 12, and 9 people per hectare, respectively.[18] Moreover, the 2016 Census of Population and Housing found that only 10% of all people in Australia spent census night in an apartment.[19] The evidence shows that despite the planning and design rhetoric, sprawl continues because, among other things, greenfield development remains the focus of profit-seeking developers, and the suburban home remains the preferred choice of most families.[20] Suburban employment continues to be "attracted to a complex mix of dispersed locations and specialized clusters, rather than to neatly planned centers."[21] Clive Forster points out that the TOD

vision of metropolitan sustainability and policy aspirations is contradicted by the prevailing urban development in Australian cities that "remain differentiated and dispersed rather than neatly multi-nucleated."[22] Given the problems in translating TOD from theory to practice, an alternate pathway more in tune with the realities of middle-ring suburbia deserves consideration.

Greenspace-Oriented Development

Our model spins off TOD, but while TOD co-locates urban densification with public transport hubs, GOD correlates urban densification with significant, upgraded public green spaces and parks that are well served by public transport in middle-ring suburbs. At its foundation, a GOD approach builds upon the well-recognized importance of urban green spaces in delivering a plethora of benefits to urban dwellers, and most importantly, in underpinning approaches for greater sustainability and livability in cities. The central spatial idea is to develop the walkable catchment of upgraded parks (a distance of about 400 m) with new medium-density infill development. The positive aspects of suburban development (such as low- and mid-rise development and access to open space) are woven together with those of urban districts (such as access to public transport, facilities, and good urban design).

Although Australia's middle-ring suburbs currently contain a reasonable number of existing parks, many of these are under-designed, offer minimal amenities, and are typically underutilized. While these open spaces are suitable for organized active team sports, other community and ecosystem benefits (e.g., passive recreation and wildlife habitat) are given less attention and, in consequence, are out of step with changing community values. The focus on active recreation in middle-ring parks is the result of the "recreation movement,"[23] prevalent in the post-war period when what are now Australia's middle-ring suburbs expanded significantly.

A GOD approach could act as a catalyst for the redesign of these often under-utilized landscapes. We base the association between urban densification and quality green spaces on three key principles. First, these spaces can provide a range of social, ecological, and economic benefits, and compensate residents living in medium-density settings for a relative lack of private green space.[24] Second, well-designed, densified urban precincts surrounding parks can offer important benefits to the utility of the parks themselves, such as increased local rates and taxes that local governments can direct toward park upgrades and maintenance, more people to activate the park, and concomitant increases in public safety due to passive surveillance.[25] Third, by being able to promote the socio-economic rejuvenation of nearby urban areas, namely by increasing their property values, quality green spaces can foster urban redevelopment and densification.[26] The GOD idea is not new, indeed examples abound in Europe and Asia of the correlation of urban density and parks. However, where GOD differs is its use of upgraded parks to leverage the densification

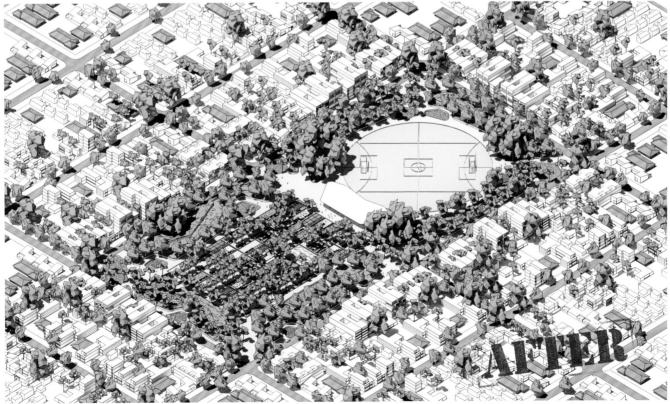

1 S. Lehmann, *The Principles of Green Urbanism: Transforming the City for Sustainability* (Earthscan, 2010), 233.

2 Richard Weller, "Global Theory, Local Practice," *Kerb* 15 (2006): 67.

3 Mohsen Mostafavi, "Why Ecological Urbanism? Why Now?," in Mohsen Mostafavi & Gareth Doherty (eds), *Ecological Urbanism* (Lars Muller Publishers, 2010), 17.

4 Georgia Garrard, "Biodiversity Sensitive Urban Design: Creating urban environments that are good for people and good for nature" (2015), https://ggarrardresearch.wordpress.com/biodiversity-sensitive-urban-design/.

5 Lin Ye, Sumedha Mandpe & Peter B. Meyer, "What is 'Smart Growth'?—Really?," *Journal of Planning Literature* 19, no. 3 (2005).

6 Simon Elias Bibri, John Krogstie & Mattias Kärrholm, "Compact City Planning and Development: Emerging practices and strategies for achieving the goals of sustainability," *Developments in the Built Environment* 4 (2020).

7 Ian Carlton, "Histories of Transit-Oriented Development: Perspectives on the development of the TOD concept," *Institute of Urban & Regional Development* (2009).

8 Glen Searle, "Urban Consolidation and the Inadequacy of Local Open Space Provision in Sydney," *Urban Policy and Research* 29, no. 2 (2011).

9 Jonathan Arundel, et al., "Creating Liveable Cities in Australia," *Centre for Urban Research* (2017).

10 Julian Bolleter & Cristina Ramalho, *Greenspace-Oriented Development: Reconciling urban density and nature in suburban cities* (Springer, 2019).

11 M. Davern, et al., "Quality Green Public Open Space Supporting Health, Wellbeing and Biodiversity: A literature review" (University of Melbourne, 2016).

12 Shane Murray, et al., *Processes for Developing Affordable and Sustainable Medium Density Housing Models for Greyfield Precincts* (Australian Housing and Urban Research Institute, 2015); Simon Pinnegar, Bill Randolph & Robert Freestone, "Incremental Urbanism: Characteristics and implications of residential renewal through owner-driven demolition and rebuilding," *Town Planning Review* 86, no. 3 (2015).

13 OECD, *Compact City Policies: A Comparative Assessment*, OECD Green Growth Studies (OECD Publishing, 2012).

14 Carlton, "Histories of Transit-Oriented Development," 23.

15 Jane-Frances Kelly & Paul Donegan, *City Limits: Why Australian cities are broken and how we can fix them* (Melbourne University Press, 2015).

Previous: Before and after showing densification around upgraded park and surrounding streetscapes.

Right: Zoning (orange) for densification along corridors and around public open space.

in middle-ring suburbs – a strategy that has been largely absent in Australian planning for these areas.

Delivering GOD

Here we explain how practitioners can achieve GOD in a staged process. Alongside discussing key aspects relevant to each stage, we use a hypothetical case study park for illustration. This park is nominally 7.5 hectares in size and is surrounded by suburban housing at 15 dwellings per hectare and minor roads. The park is geared toward active recreation in its existing state and contains three ovals and minimal cover by mature trees and understory plantings. Such a hypothetical park is typical of many Australian middle-ring suburbs.

1 Select Parks for Upgrading Practitioners need to identify the parks that will form the focus of GOD precincts in middle-ring suburbs. Access to public transport and park size are two key criteria that should guide park prioritization. Practical access can be understood as being within a five-minute cycle or a 15- to 20-minute walk (approximately 1,600 m) to a train station. Densification also improves the viability of frequent, free local bus transit between parks and key destinations, including train stations. In terms of size, parks should be greater than one hectare in area, reflecting that larger parks have generally greater potential to provide a wider range of social and ecological benefits than smaller parks. They also can be more multi-functional – appealing to or attracting diverse population groups at different times of the day and night.

2 Rezone Surrounding Urban Precinct Step 2 requires the 400 m urban precinct surrounding the park to be rezoned. This precinct is commensurate with the area where the park's upgrade is likely to lift property values.[27] This area would undergo significant infill development through a managed and coordinated process intended to accommodate a diversity of housing types and tenures in ways that avoid the displacement and affordability consequences of gentrification often associated with TOD.[28]

For the hypothetical case study park, we visualize the rezoning of the surrounding urban precinct into three zones of differing density: 40 dwellings per hectare furthest from the park, 60 dwellings per hectare mid-way, and 80 dwellings per hectare closest to the park. These zoning densities correlate to semi-detached dwellings, rowhouses, and low-rise apartments, respectively.[29] If substantially achieved, these zoning densities would increase the hypothetical study area's total population from 1,500 to around 6,500 people (presuming the precinct is 75% redeveloped at the zoned densities and that each dwelling contains a two-person household). To give an idea of the relative capacity of GOD, Perth (the capital city of Western Australia) has 420 suitable parks within the suburban core area, which means if they were developed, GOD could yield well over a million infill dwellings, a figure far exceeding infill targets. We also suggest that areas immediately adjacent to the park be rezoned to allow mixed uses. The GOD precinct's zoning should permit community services and functions such as retirement homes and childcare centers, which have potential synergies with upgraded green spaces.

3 Upgrade Parks In this step, selected parks are redesigned to increase their attractiveness and the socio-ecological benefits they provide, raising land values and encouraging an appropriate scale and quality of redevelopment of the surrounding urban precinct. Various options present themselves. Focusing on the hypothetical case study park, we propose planting park edges with a diverse palette of suitable native and non-native trees, low shrubs, and herbaceous plants so that they assume a more vegetated and diverse appearance. This planting armature following organic, non-rigid lines could swathe a circuitous promenade, as well as several smaller spaces designed to allow for assorted functions. These spaces could include, for example, drainage swales for filtering and cleansing stormwater flowing off the higher elevation adjacent roads, which in suitable locations would be designed to mimic natural wetlands.[30] Designs could also include picnic areas and nature-based play areas for children. These different areas would increase the opportunities for recreational walking, nature-based and passive recreation, and enhance the park's ability to support biodiversity. This "soft shell" of vegetation would also act as a buffer between the proposed active recreation occurring in the park's central areas and the neighboring residences, reducing the potential for noise and sports-lighting-related complaints.[31]

While the heart of the park remains open, we propose that any existing playing fields be consolidated into one space, which would be re-turfed with a hybrid species that allows for greater frequency of sporting and community uses, such as festivals and markets. The oval area's consolidation is not meant to detract from team sports' important social and recreational functions but to provide a greater number of passive (and active) recreational pursuits. The area freed up by the consolidated playing fields would be a flexible space responsive to shifting community preferences. Research has suggested that "loose spaces offer a freedom of choice of activities and more means of carrying them out," and that such spaces are open to appropriation by the local community.[32] The exact use of this space could be established after significant residential densification has occurred through a comprehensive needs-based assessment.

4 Catalyze and Facilitate Redevelopment The combined effect of upgrading the parks and rezoning their precincts is likely to catalyze the area's redevelopment due to an increase in adjacent land values, the critical stimulus for redevelopment. Studies using hedonic valuation techniques, which estimate the influence of the locality and house attributes on housing prices, have consistently indicated that high-quality parks

16 Rowan Gray, Brendan Gleeson & Matthew Burke, "Urban Consolidation, Household Greenhouse Emissions and the Role of Planning," *Urban Policy and Research* 28, no. 3 (2010): 336.

17 Jago Dodson, "In the Wrong Place at the Wrong Time? Assessing some Planning, Transport and Housing Market Limits to Urban Consolidation Policies," *Urban Policy and Research 28*, no. 4 (2010): 495.

18 Joe Hurley, Elizabeth Taylor & Jago Dodson, "Why has urban consolidation been so difficult?" in Neil Sipe & Karen Vella (eds), *The Routledge Handbook of Australian Urban and Regional Planning* (Routledge, 2017).

19 "Apartment Living," Australian Bureau of Statistics (2017).

20 Ross Elliot, "Australia's Misplaced War on the Australian Dream," in Alan Berger & Joel Kotkin (eds), *Infinite Suburbia* (MIT, 2017), 105.

21 Clive Forster, "The Challenge of Change: Australian cities and urban planning in the new millennium," *Geographical Research* 44, no. 2 (2006): 174.

22 Brendan Gleeson, Jago Dodson & Marcus Spiller, "Metropolitan Governance for the Australian City: The case for reform," *Issues Paper 12*, no. 1 (2010): 5.

23 Neil Sipe & Jason Byrne, "Green and Open Space Planning for Urban Consolidation – A review of the literature and best practice" (Griffith University, 2010), 6.

24 Christine Haaland & Cecil Konijnendijk van den Bosch, "Challenges and Strategies for Urban Green-space Planning in Cities Undergoing Densification: A review," *Urban Forestry & Urban Greening* 14, no. 4 (2015); Anna Chiesura, "The Role of Urban Parks for the Sustainable City," *Landscape and Urban Planning 68*, no. 1 (2004).

25 Tuesday Udell, et al., "Does Density Matter? The role of density in creating walkable neighbourhoods," (National Heart Foundation of Australia, 2014).

26 Ian C. Mell, "Can Green Infrastructure Promote Urban Sustainability?" (paper presented at the Proceedings of the Institution of Civil Engineers-Engineering Sustainability, 2009); Peter Newton, et al., *Towards a New Development Model for Housing Regeneration in Greyfield Residential Precincts* (Australian Housing and Urban Research Institute, 2011).

27 Margot Lutzenhiser & Noelwah R. Netusil, "The Effect of Open Spaces on a Home's Sale Price," *Contemporary Economic Policy* 19, no. 3 (2001).

28 Miguel Padeiro, Ana Louro & Nuno Marques da Costa, "Transit-oriented Development and Gentrification: A systematic review," *Transport Reviews* 39, no. 6 (2019).

29 Jon Kellet & Matthew Rofe, *Creating Active Communities: How can open and public spaces in urban and suburban environments support active living?* (South Australian Active Living Coalition, 2009).

30 Celina Balderas Guzmán, "Suburban Wetlandia," in Berger & Kotkin, *Infinite Suburbia*, 482.

raise property values in adjacent areas, but that sports fields do not have the same effect.[33] A study in Perth similarly found that bush reserves, lakes, and golf courses positively impacted property prices, but the same was not observed for sports reserves.[34] The authors further noted that, on average, the property price premium increased by AU$14,500 (US$11,500) for a 10% increase in tree canopy cover on adjacent public space. Upgrading sports-focused suburban parks using a GOD approach should therefore raise nearby real estate values. This uplift will provide local governments with greater resources for park maintenance and should stimulate redevelopment, which in combination with increased residential zoning densities, should deliver greater urban densification.

5 Decentralize Services Infrastructure Step 5 concerns reducing the reliance of the park's densified urban precinct on centralized water, power, and energy- and wastewater-management infrastructure. In this context, decentralized infrastructure could include a precinct-scale renewable energy microgrid and wastewater treatment facilities to clean and recycle wastewater from the densified area. The superficial aquifer could store such water for irrigation in the park, urban precinct, and surrounding streetscapes. Facilities for green waste collection and composting could also be made available. In this respect, the upgraded park and its densified urban precinct would function as a cell of decentralized infrastructure, to some extent free from the inefficiencies of typically aging, centralized infrastructure.[35]

6 Conduct Needs-based Assessment In this step, timed for when significant densification has occurred in the park's precinct, we suggest local governments or community groups equip the space to provide additional recreational amenities to the local community. At this point, a needs-based assessment should be conducted to establish the recreational facilities and equipment required to activate the park. Such an assessment is important because, as Jason Byrne and Neil Sipe explain, "there is no typical higher density resident."[36] Indeed, higher-density residents vary in age, income, race/ethnicity, household composition, and family status. And there is a lack of understanding about how and why they use parks, and their preferences.

The needs-based assessment should lead to the identification of a diverse range of activities and uses for the loose-fit space. Such uses could include food-producing community gardens, skate-able spaces, basketball rings, soccer goals, innovative play areas, fitness equipment, and enclosed dog exercise areas. Complementing these uses are the organized team sports that the retained playing area caters for, and the passive recreation and nature-oriented uses enabled by the park's armature redesign. At this stage, local governments should consider including a private café or kiosk to further activate the place and provide a revenue stream.[37]

7 Upgrade Surrounding Key Streetscapes The final step involves upgrading adjacent streets and connections to schools, train stations, transport hubs, and main shopping areas. Streets should be conceptualized as shared zones promoting active transport and emerging transport types, such as neighborhood electric vehicles, mobility scooters, e-bikes, and e-scooters while reducing the speed and impact of cars. Connecting streetscapes should also provide shared community facilities, such as small playgrounds, community gardens, benches, and other designed street furniture, as well as appropriate canopy cover and understory plantings.

Conclusion

While TOD principles are well established, suburban cities need complementary strategies for achieving infill development. The GOD concept brings together landscape and planning goals of community, density, accessibility, sustainability, and livability within an integrated model linking the regeneration of parkland with precinct redevelopment. Rethought and redesigned open spaces can operate as multi-functional, communal "backyards" for residents living within a walkable catchment. The need for convivial, appealing, healthy green residential environments has become even more during the COVID-19 pandemic.

GOD provides tools that bridge theory and practice. While theories such as New Urbanism provide various tools (for example, the transect or form-based codes) by which designers can implement theoretical concepts into practice, Landscape Urbanism (for instance) offers no such props for practitioners, leaving them to interpret how the theory should be implemented.[38] GOD bridges this divide. This capacity is important because globally, governance and the processes by which things get built are a major stumbling block to equitable and sustainable planning.[39]

31 Lutzenhiser & Netusil, "The Effect of Open Spaces on a Home's Sale Price."

32 Karen Franck & Quentin Stevens, *Loose Space: Possibility and Diversity in Urban Life* (Routledge, 2007), 10; Catherine Ward Thompson, "Urban Open Space in the 21st Century," *Landscape and Urban Planning* 60, no. 2 (2002).

33 See, e.g., Toke Emil Panduro & Kathrine Lausted Veie, "Classification and Valuation of Urban Green Spaces – A hedonic house price valuation," *Landscape and Urban Planning* 120 (2013); Luke M. Brander & Mark J. Koetse, "The Value of Urban Open Space: Meta-analyses of contingent valuation and hedonic pricing results," *Journal of Environmental Management* 92, no. 10 (2011).

34 Ram Pandit, et al., "Valuing Public and Private Urban Tree Canopy Cover," *Australian Journal of Agricultural and Resource Economics*, no. 58 (2014).

35 Peter Newman, Timothy Beatley & Heather Boyer, *Resilient Cities* (Island Press, 2009), 52.

36 Byrne & Sipe, "Green and Open Space Planning for Urban Consolidation," 9.

37 Ibid., 8.

38 Michael Dennis & Alistair McIntosh, "Landscape and the City," in Andres Duany & Emily Talen (eds), *Landscape Urbanism and its Discontents: Dissimulating the Sustainable City* (New Society Publishers, 2013), 51.

39 Alan Berger, Joel Kotkin & Celina Guzmán, "Introduction," in Berger & Kotkin, *Infinite Suburbia*, 20.

Acknowledgments
The authors would like to thank Robert Cameron, Bill Grace, Paula Hooper, and Sarah Foster for their insightful reviews of an earlier version of this article, and Robert Cameron for his expert assistance with the graphics.

IN CONVERSATION WITH

CHOMSKY

Is the Green New Deal a fundamental break from green politics as usual? Noam Chomsky, coauthor of the recently published book *Climate Crisis and the Global Green New Deal*, has outlined the urgent need for a global project that tackles the climate crisis through dramatic overhauls of all sectors of the economy, in line with the Green New Deal's goals of decarbonization, jobs, and social justice, as championed by climate justice and youth movements like the Sunrise Movement. As one of the world's most well-known and engaged public intellectuals, since the 1960s Noam Chomsky has been a tireless critic of US foreign policy, neoliberalism, and political oppression, which has made him an inspiration for anti-capitalists and anti-imperialists the world over. With this book, Chomsky has turned his attention to the unprecedented challenge of climate change, and charted an urgent course for avoiding global catastrophe, rooted in the lessons of past mass movements for social and economic justice. **Nicholas Pevzner** interviewed Noam Chomsky for *LA+*.

+ I want to begin by asking you about your recent book, *Climate Crisis and the Global Green New Deal*, with coauthors Robert Pollin and C.J. Polychroniou. Can you describe for readers the program of climate action that is discussed in the book and how it is consistent with, or different from, traditional green politics?

Well, traditional green politics were pretty general. This [book] is an effort to try to go into the details of what can be done, what must be done with the obstacles, and what the opportunities are. And I think the general picture is that there is now an overwhelming consensus that we simply have to end the use of fossil fuels by, essentially, mid-century. But fossil fuels is only one part of it; agricultural practices and destruction of forests are others. A holistic program has to be undertaken, moving away from fossil fuels to renewable energy, implementing sustainable agricultural practices so as to stop destroying the soil, and reconstructing urban landscapes. Bob Pollin, my coauthor, an economist, has done quite extensive work arguing, that with approximately 2–3% of Earth's domestic product [which is a lot but not overwhelming], we can meet these goals in an effective manner. A substantial sector of the population does rely on the fossil fuel economy for jobs, community, and so on – that has to be taken care of, and we discuss ways in which that can be done. We try to put all this together in a package of feasible actions that can be pursued within the relevant time span that might set us on a course toward avoiding a true catastrophe.

I mean, if this isn't done, we're basically finished. People will survive, but not in any organized form: organized society in any manner we know will be over. It doesn't happen in one instant moment, of course; it builds up. And we're seeing it: sea level rise, extreme weather events, droughts, monsoon delays – all of these have effects. In a wealthy area you can figure out ways to survive. You can't do that in Bangladesh, and lots of other places where people are just going to be inundated by the rise of a couple of feet in sea level that will just wipe the place out. And that means hundreds of millions of refugees and all kinds of devastation that you can't even imagine. It's also worth remembering that almost half the emissions come from the poor countries. The rich countries are very much higher in per-capita emissions but if you look at the total global scene, it's everywhere. So, this is a global problem that has to be met everywhere. It means the wealthy countries will have to devote resources to ensuring that there are measures that can be taken in Africa, Asia, and the countries of Latin America. There must be a global reaction, just as there must be for pandemics and other major crises.

+ In the book you focus a lot of attention on the injustices between the Global North and the Global South. But at the same time, there's this understanding that low-income communities of color in the Global North also face disproportionate vulnerability – the whole environmental justice movement was predicated on giving voice to that. How do you think of these two nested and interacting forms of inequality? And what's the role of a Green New Deal–whether global or country-specific–in countering these nested inequalities?

This is a question that is particularly dramatic in the United States because of its history, its nature. The [original] New Deal in the United States is basically what's called social democracy in Europe. The United States is a very strange country in many ways. It's practically the only country in the world outside of totalitarian dictatorships where you can't use the word socialist. In the United States it's a curse word. Everywhere else in the world, it's like saying I'm a Democrat. You know, it's nothing – you don't even talk about it. But you have to realize that this country has gone through decades of intense [anti-socialist] indoctrination. You can't pretend it's not there – it's deeply embedded in the society. It's what Gramsci called hegemonic common sense; it's like the air you breathe, you can't break out of it.

We've seen the [January 6, 2021] riots in Washington–the coup attempt–which is a reflection of deep-seated problems in this country: the power of white supremacy, of racism, the destruction of rural communities with neoliberal deindustrialization, and the lack of a cushion of social justice institutions. In Europe you have many of the same phenomena, but there is a kind of background of support that maintains the society. The United States doesn't have that. I mean, even the most elementary things like universal health care, which is everywhere, is considered too radical for Americans. And this is because of the enormous power of business, the weakness of labor, the destruction of unions, and the decisions of both political parties to abandon the working class. Democrats abandoned them in the 1970s, leaving it open for demagogues to take over. What you have is a traditional Christian, white (often white supremacist) minority feeling their status attacked, their prospects destroyed, even leading to depths of despair, an extreme phenomenon. I think what happened in Washington is another kind of manifestation of that – organized and incited by an extremely effective demagogue. So, we have a special problem in the United States.

As far as people of color suffering from the effects of global warming – it's all over the place. Even simple things like housing. When Trump eliminated the regulations on pollution from industrial plants, who suffers from it? Not me. I live in the suburbs; I don't live near a polluting plant. The poor people who can't go anywhere else live there, people who are overwhelmingly Black, Puerto Rican, and so on. So their death rates go up; they're the ones who suffer. In many other ways the same is true. A holistic approach is necessary – one that introduces effective social justice measures alongside the reconstruction of life, so that it's oriented toward a meaningful, decent life.

We see this in all kinds of ways. Take the Yellow Vest movement in France. What happened is that Macron imposed taxes on the poor. In the name of environmental sanity they have to cut back on carbon emissions. So, let's have a higher gas tax: who pays that? The people who are forced to drive long distances to work, not the people in Paris who can walk across the street from their elegant homes to their elegant offices. If you look closely at the Yellow Vests, they were not anti-environmental, they just were saying, "Don't put it on our backs, okay?" If you'd come up with the same program, but oriented it toward people's needs instead of formulated as a burden that they alone have to bear, I think it would have had a lot of support.

+ In the book you contrast that example of the Yellow Vest movement against the counter-example of a mass mobilization that includes the working class in a much larger kind of global climate movement. Could you discuss the importance of this idea of mass mobilization for achieving the policies needed to avoid climate catastrophe?

Well, the question is, who's going to make the decisions? If the decisions are in the hands of concentrated private capital, they will make decisions that maximize private profit and power, control of market share, and control of the government. Not because they're bad people, but because it's built into the institution. If a CEO decides not to do that, he's kicked out. So there must be an alternative source from which decisions are made, and it can only be the general public, the one part of the society that is by necessity committed to the public good, the common good. That's mass mobilization: organizing people so that they don't just individually sit in front of their computers and send email messages to each other, saying, "Gee, this is a rotten situation," but actually get together and do something about it. That's how everything decent in society has been achieved.

I'm old enough to have vivid memories of the Great Depression, which was, from the economic point of view, much more serious than today. And what led to the breakout from the Depression—the New Deal—was mass, popular mobilization. A large part of it was centered in the labor movement. It had been crushed (pretty much like today) in the 1920s – mainly by Woodrow Wilson's Red Scare. Unions were broken, but they began to revive, with the Congress of Industrial Organizations (CIO) organizing militant labor actions. They broke race barriers: Black and white, working for a common aim. It got to the point of almost taking over factories, and at that point the rich began to take notice; the government was more or less sympathetic. And that was a breakthrough to important policies and programs that we still benefit from today (though there have been efforts to chip away at them for the last 40 years). Well, the same was true of the civil rights movement. There were individuals who were very heroic, did important things. But until it reached the stage of a real, large-scale mass movement, nothing happened. There were ways of deflecting it; when you look through history, that's always been the case.

I think it's understood by a large portion of the population that addressing the climate crisis is a global problem. And, in fact, this is not a choice. There's going to have to be a rapid movement toward the elimination of fossil fuels, reconstruction of agriculture, rebuilding of cities, ending of habitat destruction. We simply don't have a choice. What has to be brought home to consciousness, is that we are in a unique moment of history. These problems have never arisen before. If they're not solved in this generation, we're basically done for. It's as simple as that. There are no alternatives to trying to deal with this expeditiously and effectively. And it can be done. The means are within our hands.

+ Could you talk about the split between the labor and environmental movements, and what is needed in order to close that historic rift? Is there something about the history of labor in the United States that exacerbates this antagonism?

Actually, the environmental movement started in the labor movement. This goes back to the early 1970s, before there was much of an active environmental movement, just the bare beginnings. But one of the major labor unions, the Union of Oil, Chemical and Atomic Workers (OCAW), led by Tony Mazzocchi, became the leading force of environmentalism. They're the ones who pushed through workplace regulations, occupational safety and health regulations, and environmental regulations. And it's in a way, understandable. These are people who are right at the forefront of pollution, working in the midst of the worst pollution in the oil and chemical industries. It's affecting *them*.

Mazzocchi, a committed environmentalist, wanted to push on to the general environmental problems. It was beaten back the way such initiatives tend to be in the United States, but he went on to try to form a Labor Party, which would put together the needs of the labor movement–or a reconstituted, rebuilt labor movement–and the environmental movement. And their interests are in common. Take an oil worker in South Texas: he's got a job, may even be well paid, but it's a pretty rotten job. He would do much better working, using his skills, on renewable energy: better job, better pay, save his community, save his grandchildren – all of that fits together. It's a labor issue, even more than for professionals, for example.

So yes, I think there's a lot of possibility for a reconstituted, rebuilt, revitalized labor movement, once again at the forefront of environmental struggles. I think one of the great things that Bob Pollin is doing is working directly with unions. He has managed to establish contacts with some of the major unions to try to put together programs that will deal with the immediate problem of the transition to a new economy, which has to take place, and also designing that new economy so that it has plenty of good jobs, plenty of good work–much better than today–and leads to a better society.

+ In the book you mention how in Canada the labor movement did not make the same decision as it did in the United States to forgo public health insurance. Can you tell us about that?

Yes, it's interesting to see how that worked. You go back to the 1950s when Canada didn't have public health care – the effort to create national health care was, to a large extent, spearheaded by the labor movement. Now, it's very striking that the same labor movement on the two sides of the border acted differently. In Canada, the United Auto Workers union [UAW] and others worked for a *national* health care system. In the United States, the same unions worked for good health programs for *themselves*. [In fact, it's what President Obama condemned as "Cadillac systems." Part of the reason he lost the working vote was because of attacking their health systems.] Now of course the UAW here in the United States sacrificed something. They made a deal with management, in which they handed over control of the workplace, and the management put it all in the hands of rich bankers in Chicago and New York. In return they got fairly decent welfare systems for themselves – not for the society. By the late 1970s, big capital called off the game. They said, "We're taking over, period. It's called neoliberalism." The labor movement was left hanging on the vine. You make that kind of deal with business, it's not because they're nice guys. It's because it's good for them at that time. And in fact, that was recognized, but too late.

By 1978, the head of the UAW left a labor management conference set up by the Carter administration to adjudicate problems. He quit, and made a strong statement saying, "You've sold us out. We thought we had a bargain, and now you're fighting a one-sided class war against the labor movement." He discovered a little bit late that it's always a one-sided class war if you decide not to take part. And the agreements of capital-labor mutual love, they collapsed as soon as capital said, "It's not for us." Then you move into the neoliberal period, and the mass robbery. Class collaboration may sound good, but it's not good for the society. That's a major reason why we don't have public health care. The force that's always been in the forefront of moving forward–the labor movement–just wasn't pressing for it.

+ Robert Pollin points to a role for public, private, and cooperative ownership over clean energy, at various scales. In the US, in order to accelerate the decommissioning of dirty fossil-fueled power plants, some advocates for climate justice and the Green New Deal have argued for government-led nationalizations or buyouts of private utilities and energy companies in favor of public ownership. You have described public ownership over energy as no panacea. What is important to consider in terms of ownership and control when thinking about the energy transition?

There's a difference between nationally owned and publicly controlled. In Saudi Arabia, you can call it national, but the public has absolutely nothing to do with it – any more than they do with ExxonMobil. So nationalization is not the answer. Public control could be an answer. The question of public control arises both in the political system and in the private system. In the political system, the question is straightforward: To what extent does the public participate in legislative decisions? As it turns out, very little. There's extensive work in academic political science–new studies by [Shawn K.] McGuire and [Charles B.] Delahunt–that show that about 90% of the public are effectively unrepresented. That is, there's essentially no correlation between their opinions and the decisions of their own representatives, who are listening to other voices – the ones who are going to fund their next campaign. It's not 100% but the tendency is overwhelming. So, in the public sphere, a question arises about the public's role in decision-making being strengthened.

It also arises in the private sphere. Are there ways of overcoming that? Yes, public worker participation and management can take place the way it does in other countries, like having workers on management boards. There's a little bit of that here with ESOPs [Employee Stock Ownership Plans]. Worker part-ownership of a corporation can go well beyond stocks, all the way to having takeovers by stakeholders, such as working people and communities. So, there are different degrees of [potential for] public participation in institutions, both within the state system and the so-called private system. But, as we point out in the book, there's a question of timescale. The timescale for dealing with the environmental crisis is very brief. The timescale for serious institutional change is more protracted. So, this particular problem will have to be dealt with pretty much within the framework of existing institutions. It doesn't mean we stop trying to democratize them and make them more free, but [we must] recognize that it's not going to happen in time to solve the environmental crisis.

+ You alluded to the way in which the city, the energy system, all of these major pieces of the built environment will need to be reconstructed. Designers often think of themselves as apolitical, and the design professions are not as steeped as many others in the vocabulary of political theory and political movements. What are your views on how designers should think about their role in the political spectrum, as both members of the professional class, as well as advocates for the public good?

Designers are professionals who have special skills – they're human beings who want a reasonable, decent society. They can put those professional skills to work to try to develop the kind of society that will be livable for them and for everyone else. I don't think this is very profound. You don't have to know any political theory. And in the case of landscape architects, it's almost immediate: the society has to be redesigned - radically redesigned. Everything from agriculture, to construction, to urban spaces, the nature of how enterprises are run, to where the energy is going to come from. I mean, all of these things have to be addressed. They're real problems; a lot of which are serious. Take where I live in Tucson, Arizona, it's right near a huge copper mine. Notice the contradiction. Copper mining is extremely destructive and polluting. On the other hand, if you don't do it, you don't have electrification, and you have to have electrification if you're going to overcome the environmental crisis. These are real questions that have to be dealt with. Probably there are technical answers, and the people who have the technical knowledge and understanding are the ones who are going to have to work on providing those answers. That's their duty and responsibility. Much the same is true of landscape architects. They're the ones who have the privilege, the skill, the understanding to deal with serious technical problems in their field. Technical problems are not minor. They're critical. You have to do things the right way or else you get into terrible trouble. You have the skill to do things the right way? Put it to use. +

THROWING SHADE
AT THE GREEN NEW DEAL

ROBERT MCDONALD, TANUSHREE BISWAS + ERICA SPOTSWOOD

Robert McDonald is an ecologist and lead scientist for Nature-Based Solutions at The Nature Conservancy. He researches the impact and dependencies of communities on the natural world and helps direct the science behind much of the Conservancy's work on nature-based solutions in urban settings. McDonald is author of *Conservation for Cities* (2015), which examines the role of green infrastructure and ecosystem services in the urban planning and design contexts.

Tanushree Biswas is a spatial data scientist for The Nature Conservancy's California program. In this role she collaborates with scientists from different programs to explore and expand the application of remote sensing technology and geospatial science for conservation. Current projects include using the Google Earth Engine platform to map tree cover for thousands of cities across the United States.

Erica Spotswood is a senior scientist at the San Francisco Estuary Institute and lead scientist for the institute's Urban Nature Lab. Her work creates tools for bringing scientific information into the planning and design of urban nature. Current projects address how regional planning can integrate with local project-scale design, and how urban greening efforts can be coordinated to contribute to broader regional goals for biodiversity and climate resilience.

✚ ECOLOGY, PUBLIC HEALTH, PLANNING

The summer of 2020 brought a massive heat wave across much of the west and the southwest of the United States. With heat advisories stretching across 12 states, temperatures soared well above normal summer levels, reaching 116°F (46.6°C) in Phoenix and 105°F (40°C) in Los Angeles.[1] Heat waves like this can be deadly – as many as 1,300 people die due to excessive heat-related causes in a typical American summer.[2] Most years, heat waves are the largest weather-related cause of mortality in the US and around the globe, exceeding deaths from flooding or coastal hazards. Yet heat waves are often an invisible killer, striking the elderly and the sick, putting the most vulnerable in society at risk from heat stroke, heart attack, respiratory problems, and many other conditions that are made worse by heat.[3]

Climate change is beginning to make the threat to public health from urban heat waves even greater. Heat waves in the US are becoming more frequent, with the average number of days with a dangerous heat index (high temperature and humidity) forecast to triple by 2050.[4] In Los Angeles, the average number of days above 100°F (37.8°C) is expected to go from one to two days currently to more than 10 days a year by 2050.[5] Recognizing this growing threat, communities are working on heat action plans to prepare for this warmer world. These plans often include strategies for helping the most vulnerable in society get to local cooling centers during heat waves.[6] But many communities are also striving to reduce ambient outside air temperatures near where people live, exercise, and work.

Urban tree canopy has been advanced as one solution to reduce ambient outside air temperatures.[7] Trees cool the air by shading impervious surfaces like concrete and asphalt, preventing them from heating up as they absorb energy from the sun's rays, and by transpiring water as they grow, cooling the air through evaporative cooling just as the evaporation of sweat cools you off on a hot day. But tree canopy in American cities is very unequally distributed. In this essay, we explore the results of a nationwide study on tree inequality. We argue that national action is needed to fully rectify this inequality in climate risk, and that the landscape architecture and urban planning communities are well positioned to actively work to achieve this end.

The Geography of Inequality

Recently, scientists from The Nature Conservancy, the US Forest Service, CUNY, the University of Colorado, and the San Francisco Estuary Institute collaborated to map tree inequality on a national scale.[8] Our collaborative effort builds intellectually upon a large body of studies that have examined particular cities or small sets of cities, generally finding that low-income[9] neighborhoods with a majority of people of color (POC)[10] have less tree cover than other neighborhoods. This tree inequality has been shown both in the United States[11] and in other nations.[12] For instance, Nesbit and colleagues found that across 10 US cities, neighborhoods with lower education and income had less vegetation, with large cities having the greatest vegetation inequality with respect to income.[13]

The goal for our study was to systematically map the extent of tree cover inequality and its effect on temperatures for a large sample of thousands of communities throughout the United States. We used the power of open-source cloud computing on the Google Earth Engine platform[14] to map tree cover at a fine scale (2 m resolution) for almost 6,000 municipalities and other census-designated places across the United

States. We also mapped summer surface temperature in these same communities. By overlaying forest cover and summer surface temperatures with spatial information on income, race, and ethnicity, we were able to uncover the geography of tree cover inequality in US communities.

Patterns from the Los Angeles urbanized area, so hard hit during the 2020 heat wave, are instructive. The highest income neighborhoods (the top quartile), such as Westwood, Beverly Hills, and West Hollywood, have 17% tree cover on average, as compared to just 6% in the lowest income neighborhoods, such as Santa Ana and Anaheim. As a result, the rich in Los Angeles live in neighborhoods that are on average 6°F cooler than those in less affluent neighborhoods. This seemingly small temperature differential can lead to a real difference in risk during a heat wave. One study found that each 1°F increase in air temperature[15] increased the risk of mortality during a heat wave by 2.5%.[16] In our dataset, this translates to a roughly 15% greater risk of mortality in low-income compared to high-income neighborhoods in Los Angeles during a heat wave. Our work shows that the story of Los Angeles is the norm, not the exception. We found that in 92% of US urbanized areas, low-income neighborhoods have less tree cover than high-income neighborhoods. Moreover, in 67% of US urbanized areas, even after accounting for trends in income, POC neighborhoods have less tree cover than non-Hispanic white neighborhoods.

While widespread, the intensity of tree inequality does vary somewhat. The Northeast of the US has the greatest tree inequality. This is in part because of the relatively unique form of cities in this region, with a dense urban core first laid out in the 19th century or earlier, surrounded by sprawling suburbs built more recently. Urbanized areas with a greater range of population densities had greater differences in tree cover between high- and low income neighborhoods. Moreover, cities in the Northeast also have relatively high income inequality. Our study shows that urbanized areas with greater income inequality had greater differences in tree cover between high- and low-income neighborhoods.

The Bridgeport/Stamford urbanized area in Connecticut has the dubious distinction of being the most unequal city in the US in terms of tree cover. The highest income neighborhoods have 54% more canopy than the lowest income neighborhoods, which translates to a difference in summer surface temperature of 9°F. The dramatic difference in tree inequality in the Bridgeport/Stamford area has much to do with the very different histories of these cities. Bridgeport developed as an industrial town, with dense quarters for workers located near factories by the harbor.[17] Stamford, by contrast, developed as a place for the rich, with houses on large lots sold to commuters to New York City or as vacation homes.[18]

Conversely, the Cape Coral urbanized area in Florida had a bias toward greater tree cover in low-income than in high-income neighborhoods. This unusual situation occurs in about 8% of US cities. It generally occurs in cities with low variation in population density, with most neighborhoods (rich and poor) being at low population densities. For instance, in Cape Coral both Naples (a relatively affluent community near the coast) and Lehigh Acres (a less affluent community more inland) have low population density, but Lehigh Acres has relatively lower population density and higher tree cover than Naples. In this case, there is another amenity (proximity to the beach) that high-income households are willing to pay more for, even at the expense of living on smaller lots.

The Complex History of Tree Inequality

The causes of tree inequality in American cities are multiple and intersecting. It is difficult to go from an observed pattern (widespread but not universal inequality in tree cover with respect to income and race) to statements about processes that are causing the observed pattern. Interpreting a statistical correlation between tree cover and socioeconomic status is complex. Tree cover is also associated with other factors, including differences in climate, biome, neighborhood age, urban density, the intensity of urban settlement, and other aspects of urban form.[19] Moreover, socio-economic variables are themselves also correlated with aspects of urban form, such as the degree of sprawl and population density.[20] Nevertheless, we can use historical information and published case studies to speculate about causes of the observed pattern of tree inequality in American cities. Our research suggests that one key pattern correlating with tree inequality is the gradient from urban to suburban to exurban. In most American cities, high-income, predominately white households have fled to the suburbs and exurbs, where there are larger, well-treed lots. This has left city centers disproportionately low-income and POC-dominated, and households in city centers live on smaller lots that are mostly paved.

The story of the flight of wealthier households to the suburbs is complex, and driven by multiple factors including post-WWII highway development, government subsidies for home loans, the lure of better schools, the perception of greater safety, and the promise of a lawn.[21] In many cities, racism and a fear of the unrest of the riots of the 1960s and 1970s accelerated the flight of wealthier households to the suburbs. The result has been an unequal system where wealthier households in the suburbs have more land and (generally) greater tree cover. The gradient from low-density suburbs to higher densities in city centers explains a large part of the pattern in tree cover in US urbanized areas. Low-density suburbs have higher average incomes, higher average tree cover, and are predominately inhabited by non-Hispanic white communities. Conversely, high-density areas near the city center have lower average incomes, lower average tree covers, and are predominately inhabited by people of color. This gradient is maintained over time by exclusionary zoning codes in many suburbs, which limit the possibilities for building new housing at higher densities, particularly as rentals that might be more affordable.

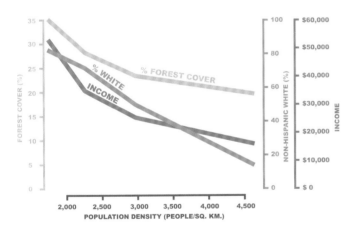

Another key part of tree inequality is, of course, the impact of implicit and explicit racism. Often Black neighborhoods had houses that were smaller and more tightly packed than those built for white neighborhoods, so the spatial pattern of de jure segregation created differences in urban density that persist today.[22] Even in places without de jure segregation, redlining (limiting the provision of house loans and access for people of color to certain areas, often outlined in red on maps) forced people of color to live in certain neighborhoods that tend to be more dense and lower in tree cover. For instance, a study of 37 US cities by Locke and colleagues showed that redlined neighborhoods had roughly half the tree cover of wealthier white neighborhoods.[23] Even after the end of de jure segregation and redlining, these historical patterns have been maintained over time, as the lack of affordable housing in suburbs kept lower-income people of color in denser areas. Moreover, poorer neighborhoods often had

1 J. Berardelli, "Sweltering Heat Wave Bakes the Western United States," *CBS News* (August 14, 2020).

2 Laurence S. Kalkstein, et al., "An Evaluation of the Progress in Reducing Heat-Related Human Mortality in Major US Cities," *Natural Hazards* 56, no. 1 (2011): 113–29.

3 R.I. McDonald, et al., *Planting Healthy Air: A Global Analysis of the Role of Urban Trees in Addressing Particulate Matter Pollution and Extreme Heat* (The Nature Conservancy, 2016).

4 Erika Spanger-Siegfried, et al., *Killer Heat in the United States: Climate Choices and the Future of Dangerously Hot Days* (Union of Concerned Scientists, 2019).

5 Climate Central, "Local Projections in Extreme Heat."

6 Melanie Boeckmann & Ines Rohn, "Is Planned Adaptation to Heat Reducing Heat-Related Mortality and Illness? A Systematic Review," *BMC Public Health* 14, no. 1 (2014): 1112.

7 R.I. McDonald, *Conservation for Cities: How to Plan & Build Natural Infrastructure* (Island Press, 2015).

8 R.I. McDonald, et al., "The Urban Tree Cover and Temperature Disparity in US Urbanized Areas: Quantifying the Effect of Income across 5,723 Communities" (forthcoming).

9 Ed Gerrish & Shannon Lea Watkins, "The Relationship between Urban Forests and Income: A Meta-Analysis," *Landscape and Urban Planning* 170 (2018): 293–308.

10 Shannon Lea Watkins & Ed Gerrish, "The Relationship between Urban Forests and Race: A Meta-Analysis," *Journal of Environmental Management* 209 (2018): 152–68.

11 Dustin T. Duncan, et al, "A Spatially Explicit Approach to the Study of Socio-Demographic Inequality in the Spatial Distribution of Trees across Boston Neighborhoods," *Spatial Demography* 2, no. 1 (2014): 1–29.

12 Zander S. Venter, et al., "Green Apartheid: Urban Green Infrastructure Remains Unequally Distributed across Income and Race Geographies in South Africa," *Landscape and Urban Planning* 203 (2020): 103889.

13 Lorien Nesbitt, et al., "Who Has Access to Urban Vegetation? A Spatial Analysis of Distributional Green Equity in 10 US Cities," *Landscape and Urban Planning* 181 (2019): 5–79.

14 Noel Gorelick, et al., "Google Earth Engine: Planetary-Scale Geospatial Analysis for Everyone," *Remote Sensing of Environment* 202 (2017): 18–27.

15 Air temperature is different than surface temperature, but highly correlated with it.

16 G. Brooke Anderson & Michelle L. Bell, "Heat Waves in the United States: Mortality Risk During Heat Waves and Effect Modification by Heat Wave Characteristics in 43 US Communities," *Environmental Health Perspectives* 119, no. 2 (2011): 210.

less municipal investment in tree planting and maintenance (as well as many other things), further reinforcing historical patterns of tree inequality.[24]

Landscape Responses

We believe that urban planning, landscape architecture, and allied fields have a responsibility to respond to tree inequality. Faulty urban planning decisions in the broadest sense—not just formal urban plans, but the collective weight of zoning codes and transportation policy and redlining and much more—have caused the current tree inequality. As the world begins to adapt to climate change, the urban design and planning professions must commit to begin to undo this historic inequality in climate risk.

A starting place might be to look to existing "bright spots," real-world neighborhoods that are green yet dense. As part of an ongoing project, our scientific team has been pulling out from our tree cover data bright spot examples that can be used to inform design and planning. Specifically, for this preliminary analysis we examined four urbanized areas (San Francisco, Houston, Philadelphia, and New York City). From all US census blocks within these four urbanized areas, we selected those that had moderate (8,000–20,000 people/km2), high (20,000–35,000 people/km2), or very high (>35,000 people/ km2) population density and were above the 90th percentile for tree canopy cover in a particular urbanized area. For instance, in the San Francisco Bay area blocks in the moderate density category need to exceed 10.5% tree cover to be considered a bright spot, whereas in the very high density category they need to exceed 5.2% tree cover to be considered a bright spot. Setting the threshold for bright spots within each urbanized area accounts for significant difference in climate and urban form among the four urbanized areas studied. In Houston, for example, the tree canopy threshold to be a bright spot is above 30% for moderate, high, and very high population density blocks.

These bright spots highlight that singular decisions, which might have more to do with building codes or transportation policy or maintenance budgets than formal designs or plans, often matter significantly for tree cover. Consider the two apartment complexes in the Mid-West area of Houston (top left), both built at similar population densities and currently with similar racial and ethnic compositions, but with very different outcomes in terms of tree cover. The bright spot is the Central Park Apartments (outlined green), built in 1976 and with a population density of 27,000 people/km2. These are two-story apartment buildings, with one- to two-bedroom

17 George Curtis Waldo, *History of Bridgeport and Vicinity*. Vol. 1: SJ Clarke Publishing, 1917.

18 Estelle F. Feinstein, *Stamford in the Gilded Age: The Political Life of a Connecticut Town, 1868–1893* (Stamford Historical Society, 1973).

19 John H. Lowry, et al., "Determinants of Urban Tree Canopy in Residential Neighborhoods: Household Characteristics, Urban Form, and the Geophysical Landscape," *Urban Ecosystems* 15, no. 1 (2012): 247–66.

20 Igor Vojnovic, et al., "The Burdens of Place: A Socio-Economic and Ethnic/Racial Exploration into Urban Form, Accessibility and Travel Behaviour in the Lansing Capital Region, Michigan," *Journal of Urban Design* 18, no. 1 (2013): 1–35.

21 K. Jackson, *Crabgrass Frontier* (Oxford University Press, 1985).

22 Garrett Power, "Apartheid Baltimore Style: The Residential Segregation Ordinances of 1910–1913," *Md. L. Rev.* 42 (1983): 289.

23 Dexter Locke, et al., "Residential Housing Segregation and Urban Tree Canopy in 37 US Cities" (2020), doi. 10.31235/osf.io/97zcs.

24 Jeremy S. Hoffman, et al., "The Effects of Historical Housing Policies on Resident Exposure to Intra-Urban Heat: A Study of 108 US Urban Areas," *Climate* 8, no. 1 (2020): 12.

25 L. Anderson & H. Cordell, "Influence of Trees on Residential Property Values in Athens, Georgia (USA): A Survey Based on Actual Sales Prices," *Landscape and Urban Planning* 15 (1988): 153–64.

26 Winifred Curran & Trina Hamilton, *Just Green Enough: Urban Development and Environmental Gentrification* (Routledge, 2017).

27 Edward B. Barbier, *A Global Green New Deal: Rethinking the Economic Recovery* (Cambridge University Press, 2010).

28 Based upon the average cost of planting, $283/stem, found in a review of tree planting costs in multiple US cities. See McDonald, et al., "The Urban Tree Cover and Temperature Disparity in US Urbanized Areas."

Opposite top: Higher tree cover makes Houston's Central Park Apartments (outlined green) a "bright spot," while The Landing apartment complex (outlined white) privileges on-site parking over trees.
Opposite bottom: The Queensbridge Housing Projects, New York City, are an example of tree cover used to advantage in a high-density development.

apartments ranging from 48–84 m2. Parking is along the street, and the extra open space on the lot is vegetated with a high average tree cover (35.9%). Compare with the apartment complex of The Landing at Westchase (outlined white), built in the late 1970s and with a population density of 24,300 people/km2. These are also two-story apartment buildings, but bigger in scale, with two-bedroom apartments ranging from 74–93 m2. The crucial difference between the two examples is that the latter apartment complex has on-site resident parking, and this amenity takes up space that could otherwise have been occupied by trees. As a result, the average tree cover is only 15%.

The observation that parking takes away space from other uses is not a new idea – many planning philosophies emphasize reducing space for cars to liberate space on the lot for other purposes. However, a perspective on tree inequality and climate risk reveals other reasons this maxim is good for climate risk reduction. Projects with less parking would encourage less car dependence (leading to less greenhouse gas emissions, a climate mitigation goal) while making the site more resilient to heat waves due to increased tree canopy (a climate adaptation goal).

There are many other lessons to draw from bright spots. Many of the general pathways to greater tree cover involve shrinking the footprint of developed spaces, whether it is buildings or roadways or sidewalks. For example, consider another green and dense bright spot from New York City, the Queensbridge Housing Projects. This public housing complex, built in 1939, has distinctive Y-shaped buildings that are staggered across the site. While public housing projects in New York City have been rightly criticized for issues of crime, poor maintenance, and racial segregation, the site design of Queensbridge was remarkably successful in achieving a high level of tree cover and population density. In this 2.8 ha block there are 1,237 residents, for a density of 44,000 people/km2. However, the gross floor area of the six-story buildings is only 0.6 ha, giving a Building Coverage Ratio of 0.21 (i.e., 79% of the lot is not built on) and a Floor Area Ratio of 1.2. The relatively low Building Coverage Ratio allows 44% of the site to be mature tree canopy, shading the courtyards between the buildings.

Designers, of course, think about much more than urban tree canopy, and we are not arguing that the Queensbridge Housing Project is an ideal urban form to be emulated. Designers thinking about shrinking the footprint of developed spaces must do so consistent with other design constraints (e.g., sidewalks often must be wide enough to allow handicap passage), and with current building and zoning codes (which may indeed not allow the same urban form of the bright spots, which may have been built in a different epoch with different rules). However, what is powerful from a bright spots analysis is the simple message that there are American neighborhoods that are green and dense, and that such a form for future neighborhoods is possible if we choose it.

Efforts to increase urban tree canopy cover must also be sensitive to the risk of green gentrification. Tree cover is an amenity people are willing to pay for, with street trees often associated with a roughly 5% increase in property values.[25] Concerns about green gentrification are significant for many communities, and some scholars have called for designing neighborhoods that are "just green enough," to avoid triggering gentrification.[26] While tree cover is a positive amenity that has a modest effect on property prices, we note that amenities like proximity to mass transit, highways, and commerce can easily double house prices, and no one has proposed to stop building amenities such as these. Design efforts should instead be cognizant of the risks of gentrification from increased urban tree canopy and work with local communities to tailor greening efforts to community preferences and to establish policies to keep people in place while ensuring that housing remains affordable. The success of these efforts depends on engaging communities early in the process and building a strong collaboration between the greening and housing sectors. There are also tools that help to keep people in their homes despite rising property values, such as community land trusts and funds to help renters transition into home ownership.

The goal must be to design new neighborhoods (or redesign old ones) that are climate resilient, protecting all people (rich and poor, Black and white) from death and injury during heat waves. These neighborhoods must include abundant tree canopy, be dense enough to be walkable and energy efficient, and yet must be affordable. This is a tall order, but an analysis of bright spots across the United States suggests it is possible.

A Green New Deal for Trees

Tree inequality in the US is widespread and pervasive – a consequence of the high level of income inequality in America, zoning patterns that have kept suburbs at lower population densities than city centers, and systemic racism in urban and housing policies. Individual design projects or individual urban plans are not likely to be enough to correct such a systemic problem as tree inequality. National action will likely be needed. The idea of a Green New Deal, a massive program of climate mitigation to reduce greenhouse gas emissions, has been circulating in activist and policy circles for more than a decade.[27] While the idea is in flux in the US, there has been significant political movement toward a Green Deal in the European Union, South Korea, and other countries. Central to the Green New Deal is the concept of economic justice, using investment in climate mitigation to help some of the poorest economically by promoting green jobs and investment in lower-income communities.

Climate adaptation will have to be part of any major piece of climate legislation in the United States going forward (whether under the rubric of Green New Deal or some other name) for the simple reason that the effects of climate change are here now, and their impacts are growing every day. Any serious effort at climate adaptation must address the linked issue of inequality among different neighborhoods. Climate risks vary by orders of magnitude from neighborhood to neighborhood, and any sensible legislation must target risk reduction activities where they are needed most. For heat wave risk, one of the most important causes of climate risk is low tree cover, which systematically affects low-income and POC-dominated neighborhoods. As part of a suite of adaptive measures in urban environments, federal climate legislation could fund efforts to correct tree inequality in order to reduce heat wave risk in the most imperiled neighborhoods. Our research estimates one would have to plant 62 million trees across the United States to bring low-income neighborhoods up to the tree cover in comparable high-income neighborhoods. We calculate this would cost roughly $18 billion,[28] which is a relatively small amount compared to the overall cost of the trillion-dollar price tag of the likely federal climate legislation. Of concern, however, is the probability that investment in tree planting will follow global carbon markets and instead gravitate toward rural landscapes where tree-planting costs are lower and a scale commensurate with sequestration targets can be achieved. But this shouldn't be an either-or situation. We need both.

Author note
This essay represents the views of the authors and not necessarily those of their employers, The Nature Conservancy and the San Francisco Estuary Institute.

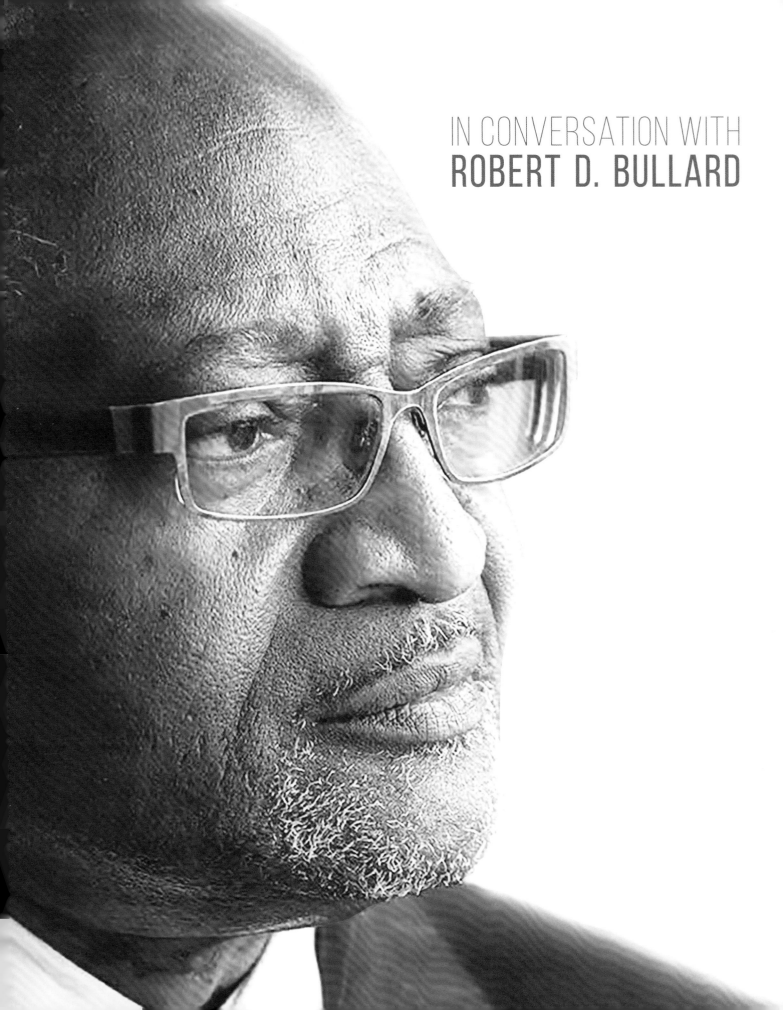

IN CONVERSATION WITH
ROBERT D. BULLARD

Environmental justice is rooted in the principle that all people deserve equal access to environmental benefits, and an equal protection from environmental burdens. The environmental justice movement started far outside the mainstream environmental movement, rooted in civil rights protests over hazardous toxic waste dumping in communities of color, and has now moved front and center in the conversation over systemic racism and unequal climate change impacts. At the center of environmental justice scholarship and advocacy has been Dr. Robert D. Bullard, who is popularly known as "the father of environmental justice" thanks to his groundbreaking scholarship on environmental racism and industrial facility siting starting in the late 1970s, and to his leadership in the environmental justice movement. Bullard is a Distinguished Professor of Urban Planning and Environmental Policy at the Barbara Jordan-Mickey Leland School of Public Affairs at Texas Southern University in Houston, Texas; his 18 books have analyzed myriad aspects of racism, injustice, and inequality in the planning and design of cities. **Nicholas Pevzner** interviewed Robert Bullard for LA+.

+ Your early research on environmental racism focused on the American South, but over time you've drawn attention to examples in communities of color across many American cities. What are some of the patterns that you have observed in your career between race, income, waste, and environmental harm?

Well, first of all, I think it's important for readers to understand that the issues that we're talking about today when it comes to environmental justice, environmental racism, and this whole issue of waste and race, was not commonplace back in 1979 when I started. My wife and I moved to Houston, Texas in 1976. Three years out of graduate school, one day my wife came home and said, "Bob, I've just sued the State of Texas, city of Houston, and this company...I'm trying to keep them from building a sanitary landfill in the middle of this predominantly Black middle-class suburban neighborhood" – not a poverty pocket, not a ghetto, but a middle-class Black community. "I need someone to put on a map where all the landfills, incinerators, and garbage dumps are in Houston, from the beginning, up until 1978 and tell who lives around those facilities." I told her she needed a sociologist and she said, "That's what you are, right?" So that's how I got drafted into this. My area was housing, residential patterns, and discrimination–I worked with census data–so I used my skills in sociology and demography, and started looking at waste facilities in Houston over that period of time. I had 10 students in my research methods class at the time, and I told them, "now we have a real research project." And what we discovered was that five out of five of the city-owned landfills were in Black neighborhoods, six out of eight of the city-owned incinerators were in Black neighborhoods, and three out of four the privately owned landfills were in Black neighborhoods. So, from the 1920s up until 1978, 82% of all the garbage dumped in Houston was dumped in Black neighborhoods, even though Blacks made up only 25% of the population.

This was revealing, this was astonishing; but when we went to court and presented that data–even though the data was overwhelming and not random–we couldn't prove that this was intentional discrimination. Now, this was 1979 that I did that study – 42 years ago. During that time, up until 1972, there were no Blacks on the city council, so this meant that the decisions about where to locate "locally unwanted land uses" such as solid waste facilities were made by white men. And they decided to place these negative externalities systematically in Black neighborhoods. But the fact that the court said this was not discrimination did not mean that it wasn't discriminatory – we just couldn't prove it was illegal (though I was able to prove it was statistically significant in a 1983 article published in *Sociological Inquiry*).

So that whole case, the legal argument of this being environmental racism and discrimination, was formulated by my wife, Linda McKeever Bullard. That was her job, to do the legal theory. My job was to develop the sociological theory and get the empirical data–and design a methodology–that showed this was a form of discrimination. So that's how I expanded the Houston study to look at the southern United States, and lead smelters in Dallas (all in Black neighborhoods), and to look at Louisiana's Cancer Alley. The largest hazardous waste disposal facility in the country just happened to be located in the Alabama Black Belt in Sumter County in the little town called Emelle, which is 95% Black. I then expanded it to look at chemical plants in West Virginia and found that the only place in the United States that manufactured methyl isocyanate was in a little Black town in West Virginia called Institute. So, when I looked at these case studies across the South I found that whether you're talking about a municipal landfill, a lead smelter, chemical plants, refineries, or all the hazardous waste facilities that were licensed by a state, all were located in Black neighborhoods, and not just poor Black neighborhoods.

I finished my book *Dumping in Dixie* on this in 1989 and tried to get it published. I got rejection letters back from publishers saying, "The environment is neutral, everybody's treated the same, there's no such thing as environmental racism." Finally, the manuscript was accepted and in 1990 *Dumping in Dixie* became the first book on environmental justice; it became a university textbook, and that's how it spread from little grassroots communities into the academy and beyond.

+ What are some of the fundamental ways that you've seen the conversation shift from then until now? I'm thinking about how environmental justice traditionally focused on local hazards, while climate threats are global. How has the rise of climate justice influenced the tenor of the environmental justice conversation?

When I was doing this study in Houston in the late 1970s there was no national environmental justice movement. The movement emerged out of protests in Warren County, North Carolina–a predominantly Black county, poor and rural–and the protests over a hazardous waste landfill. Dr. Benjamin Chavis, who was CEO of the [United Church of Christ] Commission for Racial Justice, led the struggle in Warren County, and coined the term "environmental racism." Over 500 people went to jail in 1982–1983 fighting this PCB landfill, including young kids in middle school. So, like Black Lives Matter, it was an intergenerational movement, saying, "No, you don't dump on our communities."

In 1983, the Congressional Black Caucus was able to get the General Accounting Office to do a report on waste and the location of hazardous waste facilities in the South–the first government study that actually looked at waste and race–and it showed that three-quarters of the hazardous waste facilities in the South were in Black communities, even though Blacks made up less than a quarter of the

Southern population. And then, in 1987, the United Church of Christ commissioned a study–"Toxic Waste and Race in the United States"–that showed the same pattern was a national pattern, and not just for Blacks but for all people of color. Now that's when it started to get national traction.

In 1991 Reverend Chavis convened a national planning committee that organized the First National People of Color Environmental Leadership Summit that brought together environmental justice leaders from all over the country to come up with a strategy to attack environmental racism. We developed 17 Principles of Environmental Justice, and the overarching theme is that the people most impacted by environmental injustice must speak for themselves; they must be in the room when decisions are being made. That goes to the heart of self-determination. The following year we took these principles to the Earth Summit in Rio de Janeiro. By the time we got there, our Principles of Environmental Justice had been translated into at least a half dozen languages – that's how the environmental justice movement was spread from the domestic United States to the world in less than a decade. Our environmental justice framework laid the foundation for climate justice work. In 2000, environmental and climate justice leaders organized the first global Climate Justice Summit to coincide with the COP6 meeting in The Hague that year. There we started to look at environmental justice as an overarching theme, with sub-themes of climate justice, economic justice, health justice, energy justice, food and water justice, and racial justice – all looked at through an equity lens, domestically and globally.

+ When we hear about Just Transitions, there's a few distinct constituencies that we might be talking about. How do you see the relationship between communities on the fence lines of environmental harm, communities facing threats from climate change, and the communities that stand to be economically impacted by the turn away from the fossil-fuel sector?

It's very clear how environmental justice and climate justice must intersect so that we don't somehow marginalize those areas and their people. For example, the way we define environmental justice embraces the principle that all people and communities are entitled to equal protection of environmental, housing, transportation, energy, health, civil rights, and human rights laws and regulations. Environmental justice brings them together. The environment is everything; it's where we live, work, play, worship, and learn, as well as the physical and natural world. So when we talk about environmental justice and climate justice, and when we look at the communities that are most impacted by environmental degradation and pollution, the communities that are most vulnerable actually contribute least to the problem, but they're impacted the worst. We're talking fence-line communities or environmental sacrifice zones like Louisiana's Cancer Ally, southwest Detroit, South Philadelphia, Houston Ship Channel communities like Manchester, West Port Arthur in Texas, and Wilmington and North Richmond in California. In refinery communities the people who live the closest, on the fence line, receive few of the benefits from living next door, because they're not usually the ones who get hired. Typically, workers drive in, do their eight hours then drive out, but the fence-line communities have to live with (and in some cases die from) explosions, accidents, and emissions. They are the ones who are forced to "shelter

"WE, THE PEOPLE OF COLOR, GATHERED TOGETHER AT THIS MULTINATIONAL PEOPLE OF COLOR ENVIRONMENTAL LEADERSHIP SUMMIT, TO BEGIN TO BUILD A NATIONAL AND INTERNATIONAL MOVEMENT OF ALL PEOPLES OF COLOR TO FIGHT THE DESTRUCTION AND TAKING OF OUR LANDS AND COMMUNITIES, DO HEREBY RE-ESTABLISH OUR SPIRITUAL INTERDEPENDENCE TO THE SACREDNESS OF OUR MOTHER EARTH; TO RESPECT AND CELEBRATE EACH OF OUR CULTURES, LANGUAGES AND BELIEFS ABOUT THE NATURAL WORLD AND OUR ROLES IN HEALING OURSELVES; TO ENSURE ENVIRONMENTAL JUSTICE; TO PROMOTE ECONOMIC ALTERNATIVES WHICH WOULD CONTRIBUTE TO THE DEVELOPMENT OF ENVIRONMENTALLY SAFE LIVELIHOODS; AND, TO SECURE OUR POLITICAL, ECONOMIC AND CULTURAL LIBERATION THAT HAS BEEN DENIED FOR OVER 500 YEARS OF COLONIZATION AND OPPRESSION, RESULTING IN THE POISONING OF OUR COMMUNITIES AND LAND AND THE GENOCIDE OF OUR PEOPLES, DO AFFIRM AND ADOPT THESE PRINCIPLES OF ENVIRONMENTAL JUSTICE.

1. ENVIRONMENTAL JUSTICE AFFIRMS THE SACREDNESS OF MOTHER EARTH, ECOLOGICAL UNITY AND THE INTERDEPENDENCE OF ALL SPECIES, AND THE RIGHT TO BE FREE FROM ECOLOGICAL DESTRUCTION. 2. ENVIRONMENTAL JUSTICE DEMANDS THAT PUBLIC POLICY BE BASED ON MUTUAL RESPECT AND JUSTICE FOR ALL PEOPLES, FREE FROM ANY FORM OF DISCRIMINATION OR BIAS. 3. ENVIRONMENTAL JUSTICE MANDATES THE RIGHT TO ETHICAL, BALANCED AND RESPONSIBLE USES OF LAND AND RENEWABLE RESOURCES IN THE INTEREST OF A SUSTAINABLE PLANET FOR HUMANS AND OTHER LIVING THINGS. 4. ENVIRONMENTAL JUSTICE CALLS FOR UNIVERSAL PROTECTION FROM NUCLEAR TESTING AND THE EXTRACTION, PRODUCTION AND DISPOSAL OF TOXIC/HAZARDOUS WASTES AND POISONS THAT THREATEN THE FUNDAMENTAL RIGHT TO CLEAN AIR, LAND, WATER, AND FOOD. 5. ENVIRONMENTAL JUSTICE AFFIRMS THE FUNDAMENTAL RIGHT TO POLITICAL, ECONOMIC, CULTURAL AND ENVIRONMENTAL SELF-DETERMINATION OF ALL PEOPLES. 6. ENVIRONMENTAL JUSTICE DEMANDS THE CESSATION OF THE PRODUCTION OF ALL TOXINS, HAZARDOUS WASTES, AND RADIOACTIVE MATERIALS, AND THAT ALL PAST AND CURRENT PRODUCERS BE HELD STRICTLY ACCOUNTABLE TO THE PEOPLE FOR DETOXIFICATION AND THE CONTAINMENT AT THE POINT OF PRODUCTION. 7. ENVIRONMENTAL JUSTICE DEMANDS THE RIGHT TO PARTICIPATE AS EQUAL PARTNERS AT EVERY LEVEL OF DECISION-MAKING INCLUDING NEEDS ASSESSMENT, PLANNING, IMPLEMENTATION, ENFORCEMENT AND EVALUATION. 8. ENVIRONMENTAL JUSTICE AFFIRMS THE RIGHT OF ALL WORKERS TO A SAFE AND HEALTHY WORK ENVIRONMENT, WITHOUT BEING FORCED TO CHOOSE BETWEEN AN UNSAFE LIVELIHOOD AND UNEMPLOYMENT. IT ALSO AFFIRMS THE RIGHT OF THOSE WHO WORK AT HOME TO BE FREE FROM ENVIRONMENTAL HAZARDS. 9. ENVIRONMENTAL JUSTICE PROTECTS THE RIGHT OF VICTIMS OF ENVIRONMENTAL INJUSTICE TO RECEIVE FULL COMPENSATION AND REPARATIONS FOR DAMAGES AS WELL AS QUALITY HEALTH CARE. 10. ENVIRONMENTAL JUSTICE CONSIDERS GOVERNMENTAL ACTS OF ENVIRONMENTAL INJUSTICE A VIOLATION OF INTERNATIONAL LAW, THE UNIVERSAL DECLARATION ON HUMAN RIGHTS, AND THE UNITED NATIONS CONVENTION ON GENOCIDE. 11. ENVIRONMENTAL JUSTICE MUST RECOGNIZE A SPECIAL LEGAL AND NATURAL RELATIONSHIP OF NATIVE PEOPLES TO THE U.S. GOVERNMENT THROUGH TREATIES, AGREEMENTS, COMPACTS, AND COVENANTS AFFIRMING SOVEREIGNTY AND SELF-DETERMINATION. 12. ENVIRONMENTAL JUSTICE AFFIRMS THE NEED FOR URBAN AND RURAL ECOLOGICAL POLICIES TO CLEAN UP AND REBUILD OUR CITIES AND RURAL AREAS IN BALANCE WITH NATURE, HONORING THE CULTURAL INTEGRITY OF ALL OUR COMMUNITIES, AND PROVIDING FAIR ACCESS FOR ALL TO THE FULL RANGE OF RESOURCES. 13. ENVIRONMENTAL JUSTICE CALLS FOR THE STRICT ENFORCEMENT OF PRINCIPLES OF INFORMED CONSENT, AND A HALT TO THE TESTING OF EXPERIMENTAL REPRODUCTIVE AND MEDICAL PROCEDURES AND VACCINATIONS ON PEOPLE OF COLOR. 14. ENVIRONMENTAL JUSTICE OPPOSES THE DESTRUCTIVE OPERATIONS OF MULTI-NATIONAL CORPORATIONS. 15. ENVIRONMENTAL JUSTICE OPPOSES MILITARY OCCUPATION, REPRESSION AND EXPLOITATION OF LANDS, PEOPLES AND CULTURES, AND OTHER LIFE FORMS. 16. ENVIRONMENTAL JUSTICE CALLS FOR THE EDUCATION OF PRESENT AND FUTURE GENERATIONS WHICH EMPHASIZES SOCIAL AND ENVIRONMENTAL ISSUES, BASED ON OUR EXPERIENCE AND AN APPRECIATION OF OUR DIVERSE CULTURAL PERSPECTIVES. 17. ENVIRONMENTAL JUSTICE REQUIRES THAT WE, AS INDIVIDUALS, MAKE PERSONAL AND CONSUMER CHOICES TO CONSUME AS LITTLE OF MOTHER EARTH'S RESOURCES AND TO PRODUCE AS LITTLE WASTE AS POSSIBLE; AND MAKE THE CONSCIOUS DECISION TO CHALLENGE AND REPRIORITIZE OUR LIFESTYLES TO ENSURE THE HEALTH OF THE NATURAL WORLD FOR PRESENT AND FUTURE GENERATIONS.

in place and pray" when accidents occur. And so, this whole idea of environmental justice and climate justice and energy justice and economic justice and health justice and racial justice, it's really just one movement – the one movement is about justice.

When we talk about a Just Transition from fossil-fuel dependency and phasing into renewables and a green economy, the Just Transition has to deal with the racial inequity that's been created by who has the jobs, versus who is on the fence line getting the externalities. And so it means that in moving to a green economy and a clean-energy-focused economy, we have to do it differently. We have to make sure that the jobs and benefits and opportunities get distributed to those workers, small businesses, and communities that were locked out of "good paying jobs" and economic opportunities in the past. And those communities that had somehow suffered from the negative externalities—of being just saturated with the pollution and dumped on for decades—those communities have to be repaired and made whole. The word "repair" is akin to reparations. And we have to make sure that a fair share of the resources that will be generated from this green, clean economy are pumped back into those communities that historically have been locked out.

Now we have a new version of that with the new Biden-Harris administration's Justice 40 plan: with 40% of climate investments going to disadvantaged communities. That 40% didn't just drop out of the sky. It is not welfare, it's basically doing the right thing by those communities that have suffered from legacy pollution, in terms of not getting the kinds of jobs we know are good paying jobs, that provide livable wages, and can take people and communities to a healthier place. There was no Just Transition when Black folks in the South were kicked off the farms with the introduction of mechanized farming. You had total disruption and displacement of one economy and Black workers had to fend for themselves, and then many of them left the South and migrated to northern cities. The ones that didn't go north, in many cases, had to adapt, and you still have these high pockets of extreme poverty in those rural cotton belts—"Black Belts" with majority-Black counties—that somehow did not make that transition, were not given any kinds of policy or planning that said, "We care about you, we're not going to leave you behind."

That's why many Black people and other people of color keep asking a simple question, "Will the government response to climate change be fair?" That is what we have to deal with and address in the United States, in terms of our climate and economic policies that are intertwined with our racial policies. But also, it has to be done globally, so that as we are moving away from fossil fuels and coming up with this green economy, we don't somehow punish or leave behind those countries that were the generators and economic engines for the West, so that they don't get left with the pollution and poverty. That's why climate equity funds for developing countries—green development funds—are so important. Because there's been such an imbalance, there's no way for those countries to afford the infrastructure improvements and research and development and deployment of new technologies without some financial assistance. That's the kind of model that we're talking about. If it's done right, we will improve the quality of life, the quality of living, and the health and livability of the planet. And we won't just be doing it for a few, but improving the lives and livelihoods of people around the globe and for future generations.

+ Do you feel like the Green New Deal framework captures some of that in the way it's talked about?

The Green New Deal does capture a lot of it, but it's just a framing. When you have a framework, the detail is in how you write it up in the policy. The hard work is in how you get to some policies that can make it real, legislatively and moving forward. The Green New Deal is a framing, just like our Principles of Environmental Justice was a framing. You take those principles and you give them to a body or a governmental entity or an international tribunal and say, "Apply this." And then you start to develop, out of those principles, the policies, programs, legislative mandates, orders, executive orders. That's how you make change. You can't let it be just a theory or a frame, because that's not enough.

+ Looking ahead, what are some of the fault lines and challenges that we need to watch out for, which could stand in the way of implementing meaningful environmental justice policy?

I think it's important that we understand that there is no cookie-cutter solution to many of the challenges that face this country. If you talk about our regional differences, the South is very different from the Northeast. The southern United States had slavery – legalized human bondage. The southern United States resisted civil rights. The southern United States has very lax environmental protection and unequal enforcement. So we have to make sure that if we have one set of federal laws, that they are equally enforced across the board. That's why it's very important that we have the US Justice Department getting back into the business of civil rights and getting back into enforcement in terms of environmental crimes. That's the environmental justice that we see happening not just at the Environmental Protection Agency (EPA), but also at the Justice Department. It's important to note that environmental justice has been elevated from the EPA to a direct line to the Executive Office of the President's Council on Environmental Quality. We know it's not going to be easy, but I am optimistic, because we have more people in organizations with resources that are collaborating, that are working together, that are seeing the connection. We have more universities, schools, law schools, medical schools, planning programs dealing with these issues. We have more community-university partnerships that are working on these issues today. I wish I had this 40 years ago, but we have it now and we have to take advantage of it. And I think we have to look at the fact that my generation, baby boomers, is now in the minority. Millennials and younger represent the majority population in this country. They're coming into their own. They have more in common, and they have fewer wedge issues than my generation. And if we look 20-odd years from now, the United States will be majority people of color.

We don't need to wait until 2045 to start addressing these issues when it comes to equity and justice and fairness, etc. We need to make sure that in the policies we roll out it becomes a given. There are challenges, but we have to make those challenges into opportunities, and make sure that we are bringing everybody along.

+ How has this environmental justice conversation pushed and challenged the legacy of whiteness within environmentalism and green politics? And what of that work remains unfinished?

That work *is* unfinished. That work has to continue, and it's more than just trying to diversify the green groups, which are still predominately white organizations. We also have to talk about diversifying the agendas, and grapple with the disparities in terms of diversifying the green dollars. The big green groups still get the lion's share of the green dollars. Justice is also about diversifying the resources, and collaborating in a way that we can build true partnerships. We have to talk about the green groups standing with people of color organizations that are working on these issues, making sure that money will start to flow to those networks, so that we can get this right. For example, a colleague (Dr. Beverly Wright, who runs the Deep South Center for Environmental Justice in New Orleans) and I decided seven years ago that we were going to develop a Historically Black Colleges and Universities (HBCU) Climate Change Consortium, developing partnerships with community-based organizations where our universities are located. We started with five universities; now we're up to three dozen. Our goal is to get a hundred Black universities in the country to train this new cadre of environmental leaders to work on these issues of climate, energy, housing, transportation, food security, and health. We need resources to flow to these kinds of networks and partnerships. We have to make it a priority of redirecting the flow of green dollars to follow new, rather than continue with the status quo of "money following money, money following power, and money following whites." And it's beginning to happen, but it needs to be accelerated, because the issue around climate is not waiting. And the demographic shift toward a majority people of color in the United States is not waiting. We don't have 30 years to get it right.

+ The design disciplines are still grappling with their role within the system of property development and real estate speculation that harmed and marginalized so many communities of color throughout the 20th century – from redlining and discriminatory lending to urban renewal and gentrification. From an environmental justice lens, what are some things that you think are the most essential for the professions responsible for the design of the built environment to engage with today?

I think it's important to go back and look at some of the literature that environmental justice scholars have developed, that has really hit home the importance of the built environment, and the role that planning—in some cases, lack of planning, or lack of equitable planning—has had in causing and perpetuating disparities. I wrote a book in 1994 called *Residential Apartheid: The American Legacy*, followed in 1997 by a book called *Just Transportation: Dismantling Race and Class Barriers to Mobility*. I wrote another book in 2000 called *Sprawl City: Race, Politics, and Planning in Atlanta*, then *Highway Robbery: Transportation Racism and New Routes to Equity* in 2004, and in 2008 I published *Growing Smarter: Achieving Livable Communities, Environmental Justice, and Regional Equity*. You can see the thread that planners, designers, developers all have a role in creating livable communities, sustainable communities, resilient communities, and equitable communities.

For example, you can see the impacts and residuals of racial redlining in the 1920s showing up in the 2020s when it comes to urban heat islands. The hottest places in cities right now are the places that were redlined 100 years ago. If you look at the COVID-19 footprint, the same neighborhoods that were redlined 100 years ago are now COVID hotspots, and they are also environmental justice hotspots when it comes to pollution, primarily PM 2.5. This same racial redlining is showing up in elevated flooding risks. So, as a planner, as a designer, you may now be making decisions that later prove detrimental to health or climate or vulnerability or housing. It's very important that planners and designers understand that. We need to act in a way that can somehow disentangle that legacy, so that we don't build on inequity and exacerbate inequality.

An example is "walkable" cities: if the planning and design professions don't take an equity lens, they will plan for walkability, but as the communities become more and more walkable they become more and more expensive and less diverse. We need to somehow anticipate that, to look at that with an equity lens in a way that can provide opportunity. That's the best way I know how to put it, and my writings over these many years have tried to integrate that. Julian Agyeman (a professor of urban planning at Tufts University) and I came back from the Rio+20 World Summit on Sustainable Development in 2002 in Johannesburg saying that we need to pull together a book that looks at sustainability through a justice lens. Professor Agyeman coined this term "just sustainability," meaning sustainability with justice—justice, fairness, and equity—and together we produced the book *Just Sustainabilities: Development in an Unequal World* (2003).

So infusing justice and equity into sustainability for planning has to be there, as opposed to allowing sustainability offices to do sustainability in the city, and having meetings and workshops and all kinds of gatherings that only have white people there, in a city that's majority people of color. No, that is not sustainability! The same holds true for racially diverse cities that develop climate action and resilience plans that lack equity and justice framing. Such plans could open the door to "climate gentrification" and further marginalize poor and people of color residents. We've got to have the right people from the right communities—all of our communities—in those rooms, where decisions are being made, where plans are being drawn up, where priorities are being established. It's hard! Doing it like we've done it in the past is easy, but easy will not get us where we need to go – transformative change.

A GREEN AND ENVIRONMENTALLY JUST NEW DEAL

NEIL M. MAHER

Neil M. Maher is a professor of history in the Federated History Department at the New Jersey Institute of Technology and Rutgers University at Newark. His books include *Apollo in the Age of Aquarius* (2017) and *Nature's New Deal* (2008), and his writing has also appeared in popular media such as the *New York Times*, the *Washington Post*, and *Yes! Magazine*. He is currently working on an environmental justice history of Newark, New Jersey.

+ ENVIRONMENTAL POLICY, HISTORY

The Green New Deal has recently begun refracting the rainbow. There are calls for a Red New Deal to address environmental problems affecting Native Americans. Others demand a Blue New Deal focused on our oceans, which absorb heat and carbon dioxide, as well as a Teal New Deal that would blend such aquatic efforts with the green terrestrial version. A Purple New Deal lobbies for more bipartisanship between blue Democrats and red Republicans, while a Black New Deal requests programs aimed at increasing racial equity and a Gray New Deal hopes to improve the quality of life for the elderly. There is even an Orange New Deal, although he appears to be a professional wrestler who sports denim, mirrored sunglasses, and a ginger-colored coif.[1]

There is also no consensus on what, exactly, the Green New Deal is. *Rolling Stone* magazine asked its readers this question in early January of 2019, as did the *New York Times* and the *Wall Street Journal* the following month.[2] Their answer? It depends on who you're asking. Poll a liberal democrat and the Green New Deal is a blueprint for saving the planet. Conservatives, on the other hand, view it as a federal hijacking of the national economy that will kill jobs, destroy businesses, and hinder individual liberty.[3] Then there are those who see it as an existential threat to summertime desserts. "There's another victim of the Green New Deal, it's ice cream," announced US Republican Party senator from Wyoming John Barrasso in a February 2019 congressional speech in which he claimed, incorrectly, that livestock, and thus dairy products, would be banned under the proposed resolution.[4] Definitions also depend on *when* you are asking, since the Green New Deal of 20 years ago bears little resemblance to today's incarnation.

Three landscapes can help us better understand the green in the current crop of Green New Deal proposals. The first, a simple front lawn in Washington, DC, gave birth to the Green New Deal idea that has evolved intellectually over the last two decades. The second landscape is from the 1930s, when President Franklin D. Roosevelt (FDR) initiated the original New Deal during the Great Depression. Examining that history, particularly regarding how New Deal programs such as the Civilian Conservation Corps (CCC) dramatically altered the physical, economic, and political environment of the United States, will suggest best practices as well as avoidable pitfalls for today's proposals. The final landscape is aspirational and includes a future reconfigured by President Biden's recently announced new and improved CCC, which he has renamed

1 On calls for a Red Deal see, "The Red Deal: Indigenous Action to Save Our Earth," *The Red Nation*, http://therednation.org/wp-content/uploads/2020/04/Red-Deal_Part-I_End-The-Occupation-1.pdf. One of the most insightful calls for a Blue New Deal comes from Ayana Elizabeth Johnson, "Opinion: Our oceans brim with climate solutions. We need a Blue New Deal," *The Washington Post*, 10 December 2019, https://www.washingtonpost.com/opinions/2019/12/10/green-new-deal-has-big-blue-gap-we-need-protect-our-oceans/. The Teal New Deal is discussed in Padma Nagappan, "Surf and Turf: Green New Deal Should be a 'Teal New Deal,'" *SDSU NewsCenter*, 5 May 2021, https://newscenter.sdsu.edu/sdsu_newscenter/news_story.aspx?sid=77995. David Krucoff, who is running for Congress, proposes a Purple New Deal in his campaign platform, available here https://www.krucoffforcongress.com/. On black and gray New Deals see, Chris Winters, "It's Time for a Black New Deal," *Yes! Magazine*, 8 June 2020, https://www.yesmagazine.org/opinion/2020/06/08/black-america-wealth-racial-equity; and Andrew Schrank & Jack A. Goldstone, "A 'Gray New Deal' to restore America," 15 April 2021, *The Hill*, https://thehill.com/opinion/finance/548485-a-gray-new-deal-to-restore-america. The Orange New Deal appears in *ThumblySqueezed*, "The Orange New Deal," 23 June 2020, *Wrestle Joy*, https://wrestlejoy.com/2020/06/the-orange-new-deal/.

2 Ryan Bort, "What Is the Green New Deal? We Should Know Soon," *Rolling Stone*, 31 January 2019, https://www.rollingstone.com/politics/politics-news/what-is-green-new-deal-787114/. Lisa Friedman, "What Is the Green New Deal? A Climate Proposal, Explained," *The New York Times*, 21 February 2019, https://www.nytimes.com/2019/02/21/climate/green-new-deal-questions-answers.html. Greg Ip, "The Unrealistic Economics of the Green New Deal," *Wall Street Journal*, 13 February 2019, https://www.wsj.com/articles/an-expensive-divisive-way-to-fight-climate-change-11550055780.

3 For an insightful assessment of opposition to the Green New Deal see, Kim Philips-Fein, "Fear and Loathing of the Green New Deal: What the backlash to the emergency legislation reveals about the age-old pathologies of the right," *The New Republic*, 29 May 2019, https://newrepublic.com/article/153966/fear-loathing-green-new-deal.

4 "Barrasso on Green New Deal: We Need Solutions, Not Socialism," US Senate Committee on Environment and Public Works," 12 February 2019, https://www.epw.senate.gov/public/index.cfm/2019/2/barrasso-on-green-new-deal-we-need-solutions-not-socialism.

5 Thomas Friedman, "A Warning from the Garden," *The New York Times*, 19 January 2007, https://www.nytimes.com/2007/01/19/opinion/19friedman.html.

6 Ibid.

7 For a discussion of this speech and Obama's Green New Deal see, Stefan Nicola, "Obama's Green New Deal," *European Energy Review*, January/February 2009, https://

the Civilian Climate Corps. Together, this trio of landscapes can help us build on the successes of the original New Deal while avoiding several consequential mistakes involving equity and environmental justice.

The Evolution of Green New Deal Ideologies

Today's Green New Deal began with yellow. Specifically, it emerged in 2007 when *New York Times* columnist Thomas Friedman looked out his window on a balmy 65°F (18°C) day and saw bright yellow daffodils blooming in his front yard. The problem? It was early January and he lived in Washington, DC. Sixty-five degrees in the middle of winter in the nation's capital! "Don't know about you," he wrote the following week in an op-ed titled "A Warning from the Garden," "but when I see things in nature that I've never seen in my life, like daffodils blooming in January, it starts to feel creepy, like a *Twilight Zone* segment." Friedman then explained to his readers that the prior month was the fourth warmest December on record, and the previous year, 2006, was the warmest year in America since 1895.[5]

In the same op-ed, Friedman also called for action and looked back in history for guidance. After dismissing a "Manhattan Project on energy," he turned instead to FDR's response to the Great Depression, which Friedman explained focused on a broad range of federal programs and industrial projects. "If we are to turn the tide on climate change," he argued, the federal government must invest similarly in clean energy technologies including solar, wind, and hydro power, and fund it through carbon taxes on power utilities, factories, and even on car owners. "The right rallying call," Friedman concluded, "is for a 'Green New Deal.'"[6]

While Friedman's thinking about a Green New Deal originally focused on those bright yellow flowers, in 2008 the Great Recession broadened the concept. It was also a presidential election year, and then-candidate Barack Obama pitched a "climate energy plan" that echoed Friedman's suggestion by proposing an increase in investment in clean energy technology by $150 billion and an 80% reduction in CO2 emissions by 2050. By the time Obama became president, he had begun promoting the plan as a solution to the economic crisis as well. "My presidency will mark a new chapter in America's leadership on climate change," he claimed in mid-November, and will "create millions of jobs in the process."[7] Obama then wrapped his Green New Deal proposal, which aimed to address two crises—climate change and the Great Recession—into the $800 billion American Recovery and Reinvestment Act, also known as the stimulus plan.

These ideologies behind the Green New Deal remained fairly stable for the next decade, until November 13, 2018, when activists from the Sunrise Movement held a sit-in in US Representative Nancy Pelosi's congressional office and demanded a Green New Deal for climate change. Alexandria Ocasio-Cortez, a Democratic Party candidate who had just been elected to Congress from Queens, New York but not yet taken office, joined the sit-in and drew national and international attention.[8] Three months later Ocasio-Cortez and her Democratic congressional colleague from Massachusetts, Ed Markey, submitted House Resolution 109, better known as the Green New Deal resolution. Similar to Friedman's op-ed, Resolution 109 focused on climate change by, for instance, calling for net-zero greenhouse gas emissions by 2050. It also emphasized rebuilding the economy, much like Obama's plan, by noting that a Green New Deal would "create millions of good, high-wage jobs in the United States." Yet Resolution 109 was significantly different than previous proposals because it set the entire Green New Deal within an environmental justice context. Not only should it address historic inequalities affecting poor, minority, indigenous, and other disempowered groups, the resolution stated, but a Green New Deal must be developed "through transparent and inclusive consultation, collaboration, and partnership with frontline and vulnerable communities, labor unions, worker cooperatives, and civil society groups."[9]

Two years later, when President Biden signed Executive Order 14008, the *Wall Street Journal* called it "the Green New Deal in disguise" and criticized the White House for being a "convert" to the AOC-Markey resolution.[10] The newspaper had a point. Although the executive order, which was titled "On Tackling the Climate Crisis at Home and Abroad," never once mentions the Green New Deal, it nevertheless highlights the three ideologies that had evolved over the past two decades. Like Friedman's op-ed, Biden's executive order calls for government investment in clean energy technology in order to fight climate change. It also mentions job creation, similar to President Obama's plan, more than one dozen times. There is even an entire section, titled "Securing Environmental Justice and Spurring Economic Opportunity," dedicated to ensuring equity for historically marginalized minority and poor communities, just like the AOC-Markey resolution.[11] Somewhat surprisingly, Biden's executive order refrains from mentioning the original New Deal. The closest it comes is a one-paragraph directive to establish a Civilian Climate Corps modeled on the original Civilian Conservation Corps, which became one of the most popular New Deal programs of the 1930s. But here again the reference is cautious, including only vague instructions to "mobilize the next generation of conservation and resilience workers" to "conserve and restore public lands" and "address the changing climate."[12] Which begs the question – what might the *first* generation of conservation workers from the Great Depression era teach us about the current Green New Deal?

Landscape Change and the Original New Deal

When stocks crashed on October 29, 1929, 320 billion in today's dollars evaporated from the market, 9,000 banks quickly failed, and one in four Americans soon became unemployed. Three years later when FDR became president, he launched what he called a "New Deal for the American people" by creating a slew of federal programs aimed at putting Americans back to work.[13] While the Works Progress Administration created jobs building public roads and the Public Works Administration did similarly for public buildings, the Federal Arts, Theater, and Writers' projects hired unemployed painters and sculptors, actors and directors, and writers, editors, and publishers to make art for the American public. As these and dozens of additional New Deal work programs illustrate, solving the country's economic emergency was paramount for Roosevelt. Yet it was not the only crisis on his mind early in 1933, and the new President expressed his concerns in a message to Congress on March 21. After explaining that federal work programs were essential to the nation's economic recovery, the President then reminded politicians of "the news we are receiving today of vast damage caused by floods on the Ohio and other rivers" due in large part to deforestation along their banks. Roosevelt dismissed the notion that these disasters were natural and instead blamed human negligence during industrial development. To make up for such neglect, he urged Congress to take action to "conserve our precious natural resources."[14] The United States, Roosevelt was arguing, faced a second national emergency involving nature.

To combat simultaneously these two crises—one economic, the other environmental—FDR created a host of New Deal programs that put unemployed Americans to work conserving natural resources. The Soil Conservation Service, for instance, hired workers to help farmers contour plow their fields, plant drought-resistant crops, and conserve soil and water on agricultural land. The Tennessee Valley Authority (TVA) gave out-of-work laborers jobs constructing dozens of dams along the Tennessee River to control floods, conserve water for irrigation, and produce cheap hydroelectric power. Last but not least, the Civilian Conservation Corps provided paychecks to unemployed men who are remembered most for planting lots and lots of trees.

These conservation programs illustrate an important but forgotten fact: the original New Deal of the 1930s was *already* green. So when Barack Obama envisioned a green stimulus plan to fight both climate change and the Great Recession, he was actually taking a page from Roosevelt's Great Depression playbook. President Biden is doing

www.elektormagazine.com/index.php/files/attachment/3490.

8 For one example of this coverage see, Felecia Sonmez, "Ocasio-Cortez rallies protesters at Pelosi's office, expresses admiration for leader," *The Washington Post*, 13 November 2018, https://www.washingtonpost.com/politics/ocasio-cortez-addresses-environmental-protesters-waging-sit-in-in-pelosis-office/2018/11/13/abd39c38-e766-11e8-bbdb-72fdbf9d4fed_story.html.

9 "Recognizing the duty of the Federal Government to create a Green New Deal," House Resolution 109, 116th Congress, 1st Session, 7 February 2019, available at https://www.congress.gov/116/bills/hres109/BILLS-116hres109ih.pdf.

10 Editorial Board, "The Green New Deal, in Disguise," *The Wall Street Journal*, 12 April 2021, https://www.wsj.com/articles/the-green-new-deal-in-disguise-11618267156.

11 "Executive Order on Tackling the Climate Crisis at Home and Abroad," Executive Order 14008, 27 January 2021.

12 Ibid.

13 FDR uttered this phrase during the summer of 1932 in his acceptance speech for the Democratic Party presidential candidate nomination. For a transcript of the speech see, "Document of the Month – July: FDR Pledges a 'New Deal for the American People,'" Franklin D. Roosevelt Presidential Library and Museum, https://www.fdrlibrary.org/document-july.

14 Roosevelt's Congressional address is reprinted in its entirety in Edgar Nixon, *Franklin D. Roosevelt and Conservation, 1911–1945* [Franklin D. Roosevelt Library, 1957], 143–44.

15 James McEntee, Federal Security Agency, "Final Report of the Director of the Civilian Conservation Corps, April 1933 through June 30, 1942," RG 35: CCC, Entry 3: Annual, Special, and Final Reports, NARA, 14.

16 On the overall history of the Civilian Conservation Corps see, Neil M. Maher, *Nature's New Deal: The Civilian Conservation Corps and the Roots of the American Environmental Movement* [Oxford University Press, 2008]; and John Salmond, *The Civilian Conservation Corps, 1933–1942: A New Deal Case Study* [Duke University Press, 1967].

17 McEntee, "Final Report of the Director of the Civilian Conservation Corps," 41.

18 For these final totals, see ibid.

19 My conception of landscape comes most directly from readings in cultural and historical geography. See especially Carl Sauer, "The Morphology of Landscape," *University of California Publications in Geography* 2, no. 2 [12 October 1925]: 19–54; J. B. Jackson, *Discovering the Vernacular Landscape* [Yale University Press, 1984]; J. B. Jackson, "A New Kind of Space," *Landscape* 18, no. 1 [1969]: 33–35; and D.W. Meinig [ed.], *The Interpretation of Ordinary Landscapes: Geographical Essays* [Oxford University Press, 1979]. For an informative description of landscape as an organizing concept, see Mart Stewart, *"What Nature Suffers to Groe": Life, Labor, and Landscape on the Georgia Coast, 1680–1920* [Athens: University of Georgia Press, 2002], prologue, 11–12.

20 McEntee, "Final Report of the Director of the Civilian Conservation Corps," 35.

21 According to CCC studies, each Corps camp pumped approximately $5,000 per month back into the local economy through the purchases of goods and services. On monthly expenditures by CCC camps in nearby economies, see Robert Fechner, "Third Report of the Director of Emergency Conservation Work: For the Period April 1, 1934 to September 30, 1934," RG 35: CCC, Entry 3: Annual, Special, and Final Reports, NARA, 7. On the $32 billion spent in local communities by the CCC during its nine-year existence, see McEntee, ibid., 33.

22 "CCC Also Spends," *Business Week*, 4 May 1935, 12.

23 For a more extended examination of these ecological blunders, and ecologists' critique of them, see Maher, *Nature's New Deal*, especially chapter 5.

24 On discrimination of African Americans in the Corps see, Olen Cole, *The African-American Experience in the Civilian Conservation Corps* (University of Florida Press, 1999). For a similar examination regarding Hispanics see, Maria Montoya, "The Roots of Economic and Ethnic Divisions in Northern New Mexico: The Case of the Civilian Conservation Corps," *Western Historical Quarterly* 26, no. 1 (1995): 14–34. For a critical assessment of the CCC's Indian Division see, Donald Parman, "The Indian and the Civilian Conservation Corps," *Pacific Historical Review* 40, no. 1 (February 1971): 39–56.

25 There is a rich literature on the inequities of New Deal soil conservation programs during the 1930s. See, for instance, Sarah T. Philips, et al., "Reflections on One Hundred and Fifty Years of the United States Department of Agriculture," *Agricultural History* 87, no. 3 (2013): 314–67; and Debra A. Reid, "African Americans and Land Loss in Texas: Government Duplicity and

the same today, even though he refuses to mention the words "New Deal" in his executive order. While avoiding the moniker may be politically astute, especially when even mainstream Republicans are in the habit of calling FDR a socialist, ignoring this history is shortsighted since the successes and failures of the original green New Deal can provide guidance for a new and improved 21st-century version.

The original Civilian Conservation Corps is a case in point. Created on March 31, 1933, the CCC hired unemployed, unmarried men between the ages of 18 and 25 whose families were on state relief rolls. These "enrollees," as they were called, were stationed in approximately 1,400 camps, each housing 200 men, scattered across the country. "The Nation awoke to find the landscape dotted with tented CCC camps and active young men," explained the Corps' second director, James McEntee, "in the forests, on the western plains, in the mountains, on the banks of streams and lakes."[15] Although CCC enrollees began laboring mostly on forestry projects in state and national forests, their efforts expanded into soil conservation work in 1934 when the Dust Bowl walloped the Great Plains, only to broaden once again later in the decade to include the development of recreational infrastructure in state and national parks.[16]

Such work by CCC enrollees, McEntee declared, "started a change in the landscape of a Nation."[17] The statement was far from hyperbole. During the program's nine-year existence CCC enrollees planted more than two billion trees, or one half of the trees planted in US history up to that time, helped farmers slow soil erosion and conserve water on 40 million acres of farmland, and built 800 new state parks while improving hiking trails, campgrounds, visitor centers, and other recreational amenities in dozens of national parks and forests throughout the country. All told, conservative estimates indicate that CCC work projects altered more than 118 million acres, an area larger than the state of California.[18]

Such landscape changes coincided with economic transformations as well.[19] To physically alter the natural and built environment, the Corps hired more than three million unemployed Americans and paid them $30 per month, $25 of which was mailed home to each enrollee's family, for a grand total of $700 million or more than $10.5 billion today.[20] Such conservation work was also an economic boon to local

communities, which took in $32 billion, or the equivalent of a half-trillion dollars today, by supplying nearby Corps camps with goods and services such as food and fuel.[21] As *BusinessWeek* magazine explained in May of 1935, "Hundreds of communities have discovered since the CCC was organized two years ago that the neighboring camp is the bright spot on their business map."[22]

While fostering these benefits, however, the extensive landscape changes undertaken by the Corps also involved serious mistakes. Environmentally, the CCC introduced non-native species to halt soil erosion, such as Japanese kudzu, which continues to spread uncontrollably across the American South today. Enrollees also degraded ecosystems by, for instance, draining swamps for mosquito control, and they decreased biodiversity by planting trees in plots composed of single species arrayed in perfectly straight rows. The Corps even destroyed wilderness by building hiking trails, fire breaks, and motor roads through previously undeveloped regions of national parks and forests. While such errors can be somewhat forgiven, since the science of ecology was in its infancy during the 1930s and CCC administrators could therefore easily disregard criticism by ecologists, the Corps' political failures are more difficult to explain away.[23]

Most obviously, the CCC discriminated against women and older men by excluding them from the program. The Corps also assigned African-American enrollees to segregated camps that were overseen by white administrators, and placed Native American men in a separate and unequal "Indian Division," without residential camps, to perform conservation work on reservations and to develop the southwestern United States for tourists, who were most often white, wealthy, and from other regions.[24] Additionally, the great majority of local communities that benefited financially from nearby Corps camps were situated in rural areas, where most CCC work took place, and were once again predominately white.

The social inequities practiced by the CCC were not unique during the New Deal era. The Soil Conservation Service, which reconfigured millions of acres of farmland, specifically aided landowners, therefore excluding tenant farmers, sharecroppers, and agricultural workers who during the Great Depression were much more likely to be African American and Hispanic than white. As a result, many of these minority

Discrimination Based on Race and Class," *Agricultural History* 77, no. 2 (2003): 258–92.

26 Melissa Walker, "African Americans and TVA Reservoir Property Removal: Race in a New Deal Program," *Agricultural History* 72, no. 2 (1998): 417–28.

27 For an example of similar principles put forth by environmental justice activists see, "Justice40 Recommendations," https://cdn.americanprogress.org/content/uploads/2021/03/16083513/Justice40-Recommendations.pdf.

28 For current rates for minorities see, https://usafacts.org/articles/unemployment-rate-september-2020/; for women see https://econofact.org/impact-of-the-covid-19-crisis-on-womens-employment.

29 For a discussion of environmental problems facing suburbia due to climate change see, Robin M. Leichenko & William D. Solecki, "Climate Change in suburbs: An exploration of key impacts and vulnerabilities," *Urban Climate* 6 (2013): 82–97.

30 The original CCC educated its enrollees through on-the-job training during work hours and also through after-work educational classes. On the overall impact of the Corp's education program on its enrollees see, Maher, *Nature's New Deal*, 86–91. For a detailed blueprint regarding training enrollees in a new Civilian Climate Corps see, Trevor Dolan, et al., "Building the Civilian Climate Corps: How New Deal Ambition Can Mobilize Workers for America's Clean Economy," *Evergreen Collaborative*, https://www.evergreenaction.com/policy-hub/Evergreen_ClimateCorps.pdf.

31 For this poll see, "Voters Support Reviving the Federal Civilian Conservation Corps Jobs Program," 11 September 2020, https://30glxtj0jh81xn8rx26pr5af-wpengine.netdna-ssl.com/wp-content/uploads/2020/12/Polling-Memo_-Reviving-and-Expanding-the-Civilian-Conservation-Corps-2.pdf.

farmers were forced to abandon agriculture and move to cities for work.[25] President Roosevelt's TVA, which completely transformed the 600-mile-long Tennessee River Valley, also discriminated on several fronts. In order to construct dams, the program seized land by eminent domain from African Americans at much higher rates than from white residents, paid Blacks less than whites for their land, and hired fewer minorities on TVA construction projects, and at much lower pay, than their white counterparts from the same economic class.[26]

An Environmentally Just Civilian Climate Corps

The history of the original green New Deal during the 1930s, and in particular that of the Civilian Conservation Corps, can serve as a roadmap for a Green New Deal landscape of the future. This is even more important since President Biden's executive order "On Tackling the Climate Crisis at Home and Abroad" is extremely short on specifics regarding his call for a Civilian Climate Corps. To ensure that this new program builds on the successes of the original while avoiding its mistakes, a revived Civilian Climate Corps should abide by the following principles.[27]

Most obviously, a new CCC must be more demographically inclusive. Unlike the original program, today's Civilian Climate Corps must be accessible regardless of gender, age, race, and marital status, and be open to other individuals whose sexual orientation, gender identity, and disabilities would have excluded them from the Corps in the 1930s. Such inclusivity is a matter of economic justice, since today's unemployment rates for women, older Americans, and nonwhite people remain higher than the national average.[28] The program should also be open to immigrants and allow enrollment to help them gain eventual citizenship. Finally, a new CCC must be fully integrated, without separate camps or programs for African Americans and Native Americans, as there were during the Great Depression.

As part of this demographic inclusivity, a Civilian Climate Corps must also be more geographically equitable. The work of the original CCC and other New Deal conservation programs was focused predominately on rural America, involving projects in remote forests and parks, on agricultural lands in the middle of the country, and across undeveloped regions such as the Tennessee River Valley in the

southeastern United States. Because of this geographic bias, city residents, many of whom were people of color facing quite different environmental problems, failed to benefit either economically or environmentally from nearby Corps camps and their conservation work. The situation was similar for suburban communities, which now house the majority of Americans and face a unique set of environmental issues due to rapid and often unplanned overdevelopment.[29]

Along with revising where it locates work projects, the Civilian Climate Corps must also expand what types of projects it undertakes. A new CCC can still conserve natural resources including timber, soil, and water, much like its 1930s counterpart, and also develop recreational amenities in state and national parks, whose infrastructure has been crumbling for half a century due to underfunding by state and federal governments. But the Civilian Climate Corps must also tackle a host of new environmental problems, many of them in urban neighborhoods, that have emerged since the Great Depression era. Enrollees in the new program must therefore work on remediating toxic waste sites, mitigating water pollution, and greening cities by creating neighborhood parks and community gardens.

In undertaking an expanded array of projects, the Civilian Climate Corps must also be guided by at least two groups of experts. On the one hand, trained scientists must inform the work undertaken by the new program in order to maximize the environmental benefits while limiting unintended and collateral ecological damage, such as that which plagued the original CCC. Yet a new and improved Corps must also acknowledge, seek out, and prioritize local and experiential knowledge gained over generations by residents who live and work near Climate Corps projects. It is these local and indigenous people who often know best regarding not only what environmental problems affect their communities most, but also which political, economic, and ecological strategies will actually work to correct them.

Finally, as President Biden already acknowledges in his executive order, a new CCC must focus its work on the most pressing environmental problem of our age: climate change. To help communities adapt to the effects of climate disruption, contemporary enrollees could build climate-resilient infrastructure by, for instance,

restoring wetlands along rivers and floodplains or by constructing green stormwater management systems that capture more rainfall in urban areas. They could also help mitigate climate change by helping to develop green energy systems, such as solar panel installations across the Sunbelt. Today's enrollees could even do as their forebears in the original CCC did and plant trees to sequester carbon. Moreover, all of this climate work undertaken by enrollees in the new program could serve as vocational training, as it did in the original Corps, but in this case for jobs in an emerging green economy dedicated to clean energy, environmentally sustainable infrastructure, and ecologically resilient local communities.[30]

Three Green New Deal Landscapes

The Green New Deal began with a simple, but dramatic, landscape change. It emerged from a patch of Thomas Friedman's front lawn, where bright-yellow daffodils blossomed unexpectedly in the gray mid-winter of Washington, DC. This small shift in a reporter's garden, however, jump-started a much larger idea that evolved over the next quarter century into a political policy and grassroots movement. The Green New Deal now has local, national, and international organizations behind it, lobbyists promoting it, and academics writing about it. One of its programs, the Civilian Climate Corps, also has widespread public support. According to a recent poll from Data for Progress, 75% of likely voters support a revised CCC, including 80% of Democrats and a surprising 74% of Republicans.[31]

Yet to ensure that the Green New Deal overall, and the Civilian Climate Corps in particular, are successful and just, a second landscape proves instructive. Today we drive on roads constructed by the Works Progress Administration and drop off our children and pick up books at schools and libraries built by the Public Works Administration. Many of us also eat food, turn on lights, and sleep under the stars in campgrounds that all have connections to original green New Deal programs such as the Soil Conservation Service, the Tennessee Valley Authority, and the Civilian Conservation Corps. While this New Deal landscape from the 1930s continues to shape our daily lives, we must remember that it benefitted some Americans more than others and continues to do so today.

So what would a more environmentally equitable Green New Deal landscape look like one hundred years from now? To begin with, it might have wind turbines planted across the former Dust Bowl, right alongside farms that the Soil Conservation Service replanted with drought resistant crops in the 1930s. It would hopefully include a complete reconfiguration not of entire river valleys, as was the case in Tennessee during the Great Depression, but rather of municipal water systems in cities such as Flint, Michigan. There may also be new parks, different from those developed by the original CCC on the state and national levels, situated instead atop remediated toxic waste sites in frontline communities like Newark, New Jersey, which currently suffers from too little green space and too many Superfund designations. Finally, future Green New Deal landscapes must be envisioned, planned, and built not just by administrators in Washington, DC, but through a coalition of scientists in collaboration with local residents from disadvantaged communities. Such a green, and environmentally just, New Deal not only would once again start "a change in the landscape of a Nation," but more importantly could dramatically alter the country's political terrain as well.

What is the role of climate justice within the environmental movement, and who gets to consider themselves a "green"? The American environmental movement has come a long way from its roots in Romanticism and Transcendentalism and its early focus on protection of wilderness, scenic places, and charismatic animal species but it has not yet fully grappled with the legacies of settler colonialism and white supremacism entwined with the views of some of its historic champions. Nor has it completely shed its association with a certain wealthy, elite, and predominantly white constituency. But an emerging alignment between champions of climate justice, drawing on the victories of the environmental justice movement, and traditional mainstream environmental organizations, with their reach and resources, is shifting the conversation. Tamara Toles O'Laughlin was the North America Director of 350. org, a major international environmental organization focused on climate action, where she drove regional strategy for the US and Canada, and worked to advance a more multiracial, multigenerational climate movement. Toles O'Laughlin is one of the best-known advocates of what she calls the "Black climate agenda," which pushes back against exclusionary approaches within the climate movement. She is now the president and CEO of the Environmental Grantmakers Association, which represents over 200 foundations around the world that give to environmental causes. **Nicholas Pevzner** interviewed Toles O'Laughlin for LA+.

+ For a long time, environmentalism was perceived as an elite or predominantly white concern. As someone who led the North America chapter of one of the leading green organizations, would you say this is changing today? What work remains unfinished?

Much is unfinished. I also have the distinction of being the first African American to have headed a national and international climate organization, which actually says much more about the paucity of environmental organizations' willingness to align with the widely available talent pool than anything about me as an individual. It took way too long given the history of Black, Indigenous, and people of color advocating for equity and inclusion over the last 50 years, so clearly we are failing to connect with the demand. But I think this is a good question, because numerous studies have shown that the perception about who's engaged in environmental issues and climate matters is wrong. It doesn't match the reality. Black, Indigenous, and people of color are the most concerned about climate change. In fact, historically, Indigenous land stewards or workers of the land in every capacity have and continue to have taken up the long-term care of the natural resources including water and soil. So it goes against the data and makes no sense that the protection of the environment is generally considered the space of white-identifying people, of men, or that the work is about ruggedness, rather than relationship to the land, or about fighting nature. There's just a lot of really problematic images stacked on top of each other...and then it becomes a business with the wrong premises.

It's really interesting to think that our discourse would be limited to this colonialist narrative. And it's important now to set the record straight, because Black, Indigenous, and people of color are most engaged and concerned about land and water and air quality – specifically access to resources and the overall health of people. So I think it's high time that people recognize that Black, Indigenous, and people of color not only care about people and planet, but they are working the planet, they are stewards of it. They're a part of this conversation in a really deep way, even though the work of it was built in an exclusionary way.

IN CONVERSATION WITH
TAMARA TOLES O'LAUGHLIN

+ How do you think these narratives of class and race exclusivity within the environmental movement have impacted its reach and effectiveness? How have they impacted climate action to date?

Thanks to decades of activism by vulnerable communities of every kind it's no longer deemed appropriate to look at intersectional issues through a race or a class lens. Both lenses are strictly necessary to understand overlapping perspectives, and together they tell the story of legal exclusivity – of moneyed interests pedaling disinformation and sowing doubt into a clear story of concentrated harm and concentrated pollution. On the other side of that equation is concentrated wealth. And so that story is less complicated than we'd like it to be. And it also really helps us to think about the context of harm and pollution that's led to the levels of environmental degradation that the IPCC 6th Assessment calls us to think about. It's why we can so clearly draw the linkage between our behavior and campaign calls to end fossil fuels, and a swift transition to sustainable and renewable energy. It's been in the interests of too many folks for a long time to keep the narratives separate. Some of my favorite activists have a race narrative and not a class narrative and some have a class narrative and not a race narrative. Neither is effective on its own, which is why we haven't won, yet!

If we decided to stop looking at race or class and spent the bulk of the time dealing with race, we would have the two minutes left we need to solve climate, just before we're out of time. Because it's really the thing that's blocking the rest of the work. Even President Biden's executive orders addressing climate-related risks– advocating for ideals, clarity, and investments that match–were really focused on this point. The most interesting thing that I read among the executive orders was a focus on a "whole-of-government approach" to address cross cutting issues with an environmental justice lens that recognizes that white supremacy actually crushes innovation in every group, which means none of us are getting to where we're going. That single statement coming from the White House is one of the more important revelations, because it recognizes that we're actually just setting ourselves back with this siloed approach. At a minimum it requires us to think about what vulnerable communities could do if they were brought in as partners, not only to assess the harm or demonstrate it but also to develop solutions.

+ Some of the concepts you've advocated for within your climate activism have been a "climate reparations regime" and a "Black climate agenda." Could you describe what you envision a Black climate agenda entailing? How does it build upon, or depart from, the broad demands of climate justice as articulated by mainstream environmental organizations today?

The idea of a Black climate agenda is simply making a commitment to policies, practices, and programs that guarantee that there will be Black people in the future. I wish it was more complicated than that! Along with things like the Red, Black, and Green New Deal, the calls for a global green new deal, people demanding that we finally make the connection that a healthy democracy serves people and planet because it behooves us to begin thinking about the Just Transition, moving from extraction and pollution to a regenerative economy – really, all of that is prefaced on the equitable distribution of opportunity and investments, and results in a greater number of interventions. Operationalizing a Just Transition allows us to try more stuff because there are literally more people to take it up, and that starts moving us away from the terrifying trajectory that we're currently on.

The broad demands of climate work have rarely, if ever, focused on racial equity as a function of the delivering on the call for a Just Transition from coal or from gas – even though it's really essential because Black, Indigenous, and people of color have been at the heart of this struggle, but not at the heart of that work to resolve it. Given that we've been the original and continuing stewards of the common resources, and of ideas that we could actually use to meet the challenge, climate justice itself has been built on and born of a response to disaster – and in some ways, between conservation, environmentalism, environmental justice, it's the youngest of those movements, because it is the vehicle for people who are watching their lives move further and further away from a place of stability. This generation is having to decide what a retreat looks like, managed or unmanaged. It's hard to have an offensive strategy that stops large-scale degradation when you're just trying to defend yourself. It's hard to focus on solving problems when one wants to survive.

Climate justice has an appropriate focus on responding to disaster with adaptation and mitigation. Climate reparations is a new framework, a supportive one. So, much like the Red, Black, and Green New Deal, climate reparations really lift up the context that we the people face. The call for equity is essential because that's what it would take to make any of these political actions real – which means we need new laws, social agreements, and truth and reconciliation. Having a great big abstract idea is attractive to people, but they have to go home and figure out how to make it work where they live or we lose momentum. So, I think this next wave of work—from the Red, Black, and Green New Deal to a call for a Black Climate Agenda and climate reparations—they are all responses to the big vision that provides levers for operationalization.

+ You've also talked about the need to center "the defense of Black lives, Black livelihoods, and Black life" in the work, and I really love how that both spatializes and personalizes the challenge, and maybe also points to some of the disconnect of the more myopically carbon-focused agendas. What is an initiative you're excited about, that you think will be important for reshaping the relationship to environmentalism, or to climate action, for communities of color?

Yes, it does expose the disconnect. It takes you right to the heart of where well-intentioned silos keep out the good stuff. It's like an antibiotic—it kills a lot of bad stuff, but it kills some of the good stuff too. And at this point we've killed too many things to keep continuing the regimen of responses.

I'm really excited about the global campaign for a Fossil Fuel Non-Proliferation Treaty—styled after the work of nuclear non-proliferation—because it sets forth a pathway with tools to commence the Just Transition. It responds to the dead letter that is the Paris Agreement, without having to go through another dead-letter process of getting an amendment. I'm excited that it has a global registry of fossil fuel reserves and production, which can provide an open-source ability to hold governments accountable, at scale, for their role in setting the market for energy and in fossil fuel production. It's the only campaign among the many that I have been involved in that is focused on the supply side and can be allied with things like climate reparations or a global green new deal, because it gives them teeth.

Everybody can yell about the Just Transition, but if you ask people, "How are we going to do it? Who's going to start? What do we do? How does it happen?" – if you talk to someone in Saudi Arabia, they might see fossil fuels as a line of defense against external governments around the world, because having capital means you can at least fight for your own way of life. So, I do think the Just Transition needs to not just be about 77,000 American coal miners, but should be a global conversation. I like the fact that the non-proliferation campaign is coming from the Global South, that it's thinking about all the different places where the challenge of moving away from extraction and pollution shows up. It is a response offering open-source solutions, regional and local opportunities for people to sign on at the level of the municipality and push through their own government, and it supports the recognition of existing treaties. Because you can't support the Fossil Fuel Non-Proliferation Treaty if you don't support the concept of government sovereignty or treaties. It's the same idea with climate reparations: you can't argue for the end of the concentration of pollution and harm, if in general, you don't believe that people should get care and repair when they've been hurt.

The open-source global part of the Fossil Fuel Non-Proliferation Treaty is similar to operations in the world of cryptocurrency (which I have many problems with, for extractive reasons and others), but it's attractive to connect the change to an open-source ledger of all the things that are killing your future economy and destroying your health. It would make it a heck of a lot easier to develop a roadmap of what should be knocked down first in a way that allows people to make shifts, to make changes, to manage the retreat from careers that are extractive into ones that are not. Of all of the ideas, it's the one that has multiple prongs and things that could be actualized right now without people going back to processes that didn't work, because it immediately uses the technology we have and recognizes that people are very aware of what's causing them harm. If we started to look at harm as the determinant for how to handle the Just Transition, suddenly it becomes easier to say, "Okay, we need to close these three things, and then these two things, and then this one thing," as opposed to having it be an abstract set of concepts, where people just volunteer and stop being effective in ways they know how to be, and take risks that they're not prepared to take.

+ What do you think some of the issues are that are most essential for designers as professionals responsible for the design of the built environment to engage with today, and how might designers play a more constructive role in the initiatives that you consider the most urgent?

Well, first I'd say, as a practitioner you always have to take a deep breath and recognize your own humanity. It helps with all the other stuff, because once your training kicks in the context can feel like it happens in separate boxes. Next, I think it's really important to recognize that the context we are all sitting in, regardless of what we're looking at, is one where legal apartheid, from segregationism in city planning and urban design to racially restrictive covenants to predatory zoning and lending, has cemented the exclusion and harm that made it so that Black, Indigenous, and people of color in their own communities are faced with a nonstop and continuing legacy that has to be met with redesign. So, some of it is just looking at the scale and scope of what we have to deal with: the idea that we have to continually train ourselves–or retrain ourselves–to respond with redesign that focuses on equity and care and repair at the center of any solution that gets built.

The design disciplines really have to think about restorative frameworks for their analysis. Ask what is the restorative framework that responds to the problem that's in front of you, and then think about who's in the plan and who isn't. You are really asking the question, "Is what I'm doing a gate opening or a gate closing activity?" So that means responding with a shift in values. That's ultimately what we're talking about: an assessment of assets–or reassessment of assets–and really starting to question who decides what is valuable, and to whom does that matter, and for what purposes, both now and later. I also think that that means thinking about what it would mean to build (or rebuild) a robust aptitude for partnership in the ways that allow Black, Indigenous, and people of color as communities and individuals in communities to be a part of rebuilding infrastructure, and how place-based solutions and energy imperatives have to be woven through all of that.

I think it's really a matter of stepping back from what we know to be true, and trying to figure out who could this hurt, and why might that happen. In terms of the challenge of decarbonization, as a practitioner you might show up and think, I want my work to be an integrated solution to decarbonize, among other values, and I want people to feel like this thing is safe. Well, safe for whom? In what context? What does it mean if the safety you envisage locally requires us to bring in materials that might cause harm elsewhere in the way they're produced (as we've learned can be the case with the lithium or cobalt in batteries, for example), and we don't care about where those materials are coming from, and haven't thought about it from the point of view of a life-cycle process, or a multi-generational waste process.

I don't believe that there are people that build things that aren't thinking about entire worlds. So why not just open up the vision, make the context of a project more appropriate for the people who will live their lives throughout all of these shifts? If the thing is built to last 100 years, what will those people look like? What will they need to survive? It's part of the reason I'm constantly telling people to read Vanessa Keith's *2100: A Dystopian Utopia* (2017). Not just because I like the cool graphics, but because I think we have to start opening up the work to make what we do today matter tomorrow. What is managed retreat going to look like? Who will have to live with flooding all the time or move? Who will have to live with fires all the time or flee? Who will the new nomads be and what kinds of needs will they have? I think we are running away from the empowerment that could happen if design took this up. All industries have questions to answer, but designers are visionary – so maybe they should do just that.

1 Jariel Arvin, "The Urgency of the Black Climate Agenda," *Vox.com* (April 7, 2021).

2 See, e.g., Matthew Ballew, et al., "Which Racial/Ethnic Groups Care Most About Climate Change?" *Yale Program on Climate Change Communication* (April 16, 2020); Chris Mooney & Peyton Craighill, "Why do Black and Latino Americans Support Climate Action So Much More than Whites?" *Washington Post* (December 1, 2014).

PEDER ANKER

Peder Anker is a professor of the history of science at New York University. He is the author of several books on environmental history and ecological design, including *From Bauhaus to Eco-House: A History of Ecological Design* (2010) and *Global Design: Elsewhere Envisioned* (2014). His latest book is *The Power of the Periphery: How Norway Became an Environmental Pioneer for the World* (2020).

+ ENVIRONMENTAL HUMANITIES

"It is the Noah's Ark for securing biological diversity for future generations," Norway's Prime Minister Jens Stoltenberg told a freezing audience of world dignitaries.[1] The occasion was the opening of the Svalbard Global Seed Vault in February 2008, a vault constructed to secure the world's food crops against climate change, wars, and natural disasters. The seed vault was to be a safe deposit box for the world's genetic material, secured in eternal permafrost high above the coastline to protect against climate-change-induced sea level rise. In this icy Arctic facility, national seed banks from all over the world could deposit their genetic heritage under Norwegian protection. After unlocking the vault, the 2004 Nobel Peace Prize–winner Wangari Maathai of Kenya made the first deposit: a box of Kenyan rice seeds. For developing countries, it was especially important that deposits in the vault could only be accessed by the seeds' owners, particularly since seed industries had a habit of reaping the benefits of their nations' genetic heritage without consent.[2] Norway was to be on the good side of such conflicts by constructing the vault to protect the vulnerable, rather than enrich the strong. In effect, Norwegians assumed the role of bank vault executives for the economy of nature.

"Doomsday Seed Vault" and "Noah's Seed Ark" were the nicknames suggested to the press by the Norwegian government. They were told that Norway had financed and built the vault simply "as a service to the world community."[3] The opening ceremony became a major news item in media outlets around the world, often as front-page news, with Norwegians portrayed as virtuous guardians of the world's biological heritage. These articles had a biblical ring to them: the oceans were rising while Stoltenberg was depicted as the world's Noah: securing at least two seeds of every living species in his ark. The dramatic architectural design of the seed vault's entrance (by Peter W. Søderman) provided a perfect setting for the event, with a large, perpetually glowing crystal window in a landscape engulfed in the Arctic dark.

Norway had an underlying political interest in building a presence in the remote archipelago of Svalbard. Since the islands were annexed back in 1920 in the context of the nation's imperial ambitions, Norway has done its best to confirm its sovereignty. Most countries in the northern hemisphere are signatories to the Spitsbergen Treaty of 1920 establishing Norwegian dominion over the Svalbard Archipelago; however, many countries of the Global South (including Kenya) are yet to sign. The backdrop of building the seed vault on Spitsbergen was thus to showcase to the world– especially to the Global South–the virtue of Norwegian sovereignty over these Arctic islands. Be that as it may, it would be too cynical to argue that the *only* purpose of the vault was geopolitical –

1 Doug Mellgren, "'Doomsday seed vault' opens in Arctic," *NBC News* (February 27, 2008), http://www.nbcnews.com/id/23352014/ns/technology_and_science-science/t/doomsday-seed-vault-opens-arctic/#.VXh0tTtFBhE.

2 Hanne Svarstad & Shivcharn S. Dhillion (eds), *Responding to Bioprospecting* (Spartacus, 2000).

3 Svalbard Global Seed Vault, "'Doomsday Seed Vault' to Open in Arctic Circle on February 26th" https://www.croptrust.org/wp-content/uploads/2014/12/SGSV-Media-Advisory-FINAL-ENG.pdf; Marte Qvenild, "Svalbard Global Seed Vault: a 'Noah's Ark' for the world's seeds," Development in Practice 18, no. 1 (2008): 110–16.

4 Anderson Cooper, "Alexandria Ocasio-Cortez on 60 Minutes," CBS (January 6, 2019); Bill McKibben, *Falter: Has the Human Game Begun to Play Itself Out?* (Henry Holt & Co., 2019), 116, 193; Anu Partanen, *The Nordic Theory of Everything: A Search of a Better Life* (Harper Collins, 2016).

5 Quotes by Jan Egeland (1985) and Jonas Gahr Støre (2006), respectively Norway's State Secretary and Minister of Foreign Affairs, in Øyvind Østerud, "Lite land som humanitær stormakt?" *Nytt norsk tidsskrift* 4 (2006): 303–16. Helge Pharo, "Norway's Peace Tradition Spanning 100 Years," *Scandinavian Review* 93 (2005): 15–23.

6 Edward W. Said, "How do you spell Apartheid? O-s-l-o" *Ha'aretz* (October 11, 1998).

7 World Commission on Environment and Development, *Our Common Future* (Oxford University Press, 1987).

8 Arne Johan Vetlesen, *The Denial of Nature: Environmental Philosophy in the Era of Global Capitalism* (Taylor & Francis, 2015).

Stoltenberg genuinely wanted Norway to do something good for the world, and the vault was a high profile and relatively easy way of achieving just that. It is also a classic example of design playing along.

Norwegians like to think of Norway as being an environmentally sound nation; like the Global Seed Vault itself, a beacon of virtue. They fashion themselves and their country as a microcosm for a better macrocosm. In the United States, Norwegians have met a receptive audience, especially among activists on the progressive left who tend to admire everything Scandinavian. For example, when US Congresswoman Alexandria Ocasio-Cortez promoted a Green New Deal in an interview for CBS's *60 Minutes*, she pointed to Scandinavia and Norway as exemplars of environmental socialism.[4] In doing so, she appealed to a deep-seated longing for the politics of this region among her audience.

The official foreign policy of Norway is to establish the tiny nation as a "humanitarian superpower" and a "peace nation."[5] This goes back to the Oslo Accord of 1995 between Palestine and Israel and is consolidated every year when the world's dignitaries come to Oslo to solemnly witness the ultimate peace fest hosted by the Permanent Secretariat of the Nobel Peace Prize.[6] Similarly, the national policy has been to put the country on the diplomatic map by empowering its politicians to take the lead in international negotiations and in doing so bolster the image of Norway as the world's environmental leader. Norwegian Prime Minister Gro Harlem Brundtland's 1987 *Our Common Future* report is a prime example. It laid out the principles for sustainable development, and by inference, if not in fact, established Norway as the gold standard in how to reach them.[7] This trend continued with Prime Minister Stoltenberg who, in his capacity as the United Nations Special Envoy on Climate Change, points to Norway as an exemplar of sustainability and climate leadership. More generally, scholar-activists in Norway have, since the 1970s, presented to the world various philosophies of global environmental improvement, including deep ecology, biocentrism, eco-politics, eco-theology, sustainability, carbon emission trading, and more. The expression "Scandinavian design" is no exception to this trend, as it works to combine the rationality of modernism with the vernacular attributes of homegrown environmental sensitivity. Famous Norwegian architects and firms from Magnus Poulsson, to Arne Korsmo, Sverre Fehn, and Snøhetta also share this aspiration. Indeed, environmental sensitivity is the common theme in Norwegian architectural history and current affairs.

Yet this beneficent environmental gaze on the world did not necessarily lead to sound environmental policies at home. A leading Norwegian environmental ethicist rightly notes that "there is very little to be proud about" with respect to environmental protection in Norway.[8] The high ideals of sustainability may have captured the longings of the nation, but they have not so easily transferred into practical politics or behaviors of everyday life. The pushback from industrialists and the powerful oil lobby has been considerable and many anti-environmental practices continue unabated. Some examples of such practices include the hunting of whales, harp seal pups, wolves, bears, and lynx; the dumping of toxic mining waste in the fjords; overfishing; pollution caused by salmon aquaculture and industrial farming; the construction of hydro-power dams; the commercialization of nature reserves; and, more recently, the building of wind turbines and electric transmission lines in wilderness areas. Not to mention the day-to-day politics of pumping as much petroleum as possible from the nation's numerous oil rigs despite knowing that this contributes directly to climate change.

To signal a shift in a greener direction, the state's petroleum company, Statoil, recently changed its name to Equinor, sold its holdings in Canadian polluting tar-sands, and began investing in offshore wind power. Although these initiatives have taken center stage in the company's rebranding, Equinor has increased its petroleum production from oil fields in the vulnerable Barents Sea in the Arctic, as well as in Algeria, Angola, Azerbaijan, Brazil, Canada, Nigeria, and more. Following the money of a rich nation on an environmental mission of bettering the world is also instructive. Take, for example, the significant funds used to purchase Clean Development Mechanism certificates, which initiated emission-reduction projects in the Global South to be counted as greenhouse gas emission reduction in Norway.[9] And it is hard to find critical literature about the international investments of the nation's prime owner of "green" hydro-electric power, Statkraft (state power). Its various developments in the wilderness of countries like Nepal, India, Brazil, Chile, and Peru have hardly been questioned in Norway. The point is not to insinuate conspiracy or even that the truth is hidden from Norwegian citizens, but instead to note that the Norwegian self-understanding of being environmentally good to the world creates a certain form of national self-righteousness and complacency that hinders critical investigation into what is actually going on.[10]

"Climate hypocrites" is how CNN recently portrayed Norway by pointing to the paradox of the nation's petroleum financing

9 Erik Martiniussen, *Drivhuseffekten: Klimapolitikken som forsvant* (Manifest, 2013).

10 Norway's $2.6 billion contribution to the International Climate and Forest Initiative to save the world's tropical rainforests may well be the exception that proves the rule. Following investigation, the Office of the Auditor General evaluated the initiative as being largely ineffective and marred by corruption and fraud: Riksrevisjonen, *The Office of the Auditor General of Norway's Investigation of Norway's International Climate and Forest Initiative* (Fagbokforlaget, 2019), 7–8.

11 Ivana Kottasova, "Norway, the UK and Canada are not climate champions. They are climate hypocrites," *CNN* (February 17, 2021).

12 Lan Marie Nguyen Berg, Deputy Mayor of Transport and Environment in Oslo, quoted in Jonathan Watts, "Norway's Push for Arctic Oil and Gas Threatens Paris Climate Goals," *The Guardian* (August 10, 2017).

13 Bill McKibben, *Twitter* @billmckibben (March 8, 2019).

14 Kari Marie Norgaard, *Living in Denial: Climate Change, Emotions and Everyday Life* (MIT Press, 2011).

15 Morten A. Strøksnes, *Shark Drunk: The Art of Catching a Large Shark from a Tiny Rubber Dinghy in a Big Ocean* (Knopf, 2017); Lars Mytting, *Norwegian Wood: Chopping, Stacking, and Drying Wood the Scandinavian Way* (Abrams Image, 2015); NRK/Netflix, *National Firewood Night* (2013).

16 Dag Hessen, *Landskap i Endring* (Pax, 2016), 7.

environmentalism.[11] The environmental activists who make up the small Green Party in Norway could not agree more. By speaking truth to power, Green Party leaders have made it clear that they want to stop the greenwashing. In the words of their most well-known representative, they "don't want to support a government that continues to explore new oil. That would be hypocrisy."[12] Standing up in this way to the nation's powerful petroleum lobby has led the Parliament to decide that the massive Government Pension Fund of Norway should divest from fossil fuels and invest more in renewable energy. This decision was picked up by major news outlets and environmental NGOs around the world, as the fund is the world's largest with over US$1.15 trillion in assets, including 1.5% of all stocks globally. "Huge, huge, huge win" for the divest movement, the founder of 350.org, Bill McKibben, tweeted to a largely American audience fed up with then-President Donald Trump's environmental policies.[13] As it turns out, the fine print of the Norwegian divestment plan was murky. Yet in the divided climate politics of the US—which are framed by binaries similar to those of the Cold War—it was a beacon of good news and an example to admire for Green New Deal advocates. Norwegian politicians tapped into a tradition in Norway to seek to shine as the world's green do-gooders, powered by the money from the oil.

In the powerful Oslo Municipality, the Green Party is in a power-broker position and they have sought to take the nation's capital in a more sustainable direction. They have managed to enforce an environmental regime which is anything but symbolic, leading up to the city being awarded the European Green Capital of 2019. They are on track to turn Oslo into the first carbon neutral city in the world by 2030. This marks a positive shift away from environmentalism only being located within the foreign policy domain. Thanks to the Green Party, Norway has slowly begun to not only talk the talk but also walk the walk.

The question remains, however, how do we explain the Norwegian paradox of seeking to be environmentally sensitive while continuing to profit from polluting the world? How was the greenwashing of an entire nation possible? The answer lies in the national character: most Norwegians are perfectly comfortable using oil paint to color their nation in various shades of green. The way in which Norwegians individually learn to reconcile Norway's split personality is played out across the nation's landscape. For example, vacationing in remote mountain and fjord cottages is at the heart of Norwegian social life and the very core of Norwegian identity. Ask a Norwegian about their life in their cabin and you will be able to build an image of their deepest dreams and desires. As they see it, life and nature well beyond the city is morally superior and the source of everything good. When COVID-19 hit Norway and the government-imposed stay-at-home orders that prohibited travel to cabins, it was the equivalent of denying coastal Californians access to their beaches or American evangelicals access to church services. This national longing for nature in the remote is the key to understanding the paradoxical Norwegian approach to environmental issues: the pristine periphery serves in environmental debates as the model for the dirty center in need of change. The nation's psychological condition can be mapped along a transect: mountains of virtue at one end and the polluted city in a valley at the other.

Environmentalists, however, would likely readily admit that people actually living in Norway's remote areas are not necessarily green idealists. As Kari Marie Norgaard has shown, the lives of those in small-town Norway are often far from ecologically self-sufficient, with many people living in denial of climate change.[14] Yet the imagined life of Norway's fishermen-peasants still serves as an image of environmental self-sufficiency. Such identity is constantly reinforced in Norwegian popular culture: some of Norway's bestselling cultural exports in recent years include a memoir about catching large sharks in the pristine Norwegian Arctic archipelago of Vesterålen; a guide on chopping, stacking, and drying firewood the "Scandinavian way"; and a six-hour "slow TV" special on how to maintain a crackling fireplace.[15] The simple life in remote places evokes a deep-seated Norwegian nostalgia. The dualism that lies at the heart of Norwegian identity is captured perfectly by biologist Dag Hessen, who wrote: "Soon Norway will not have any farmers and fishermen left, yet we are still a land of farmers and fishermen."[16]

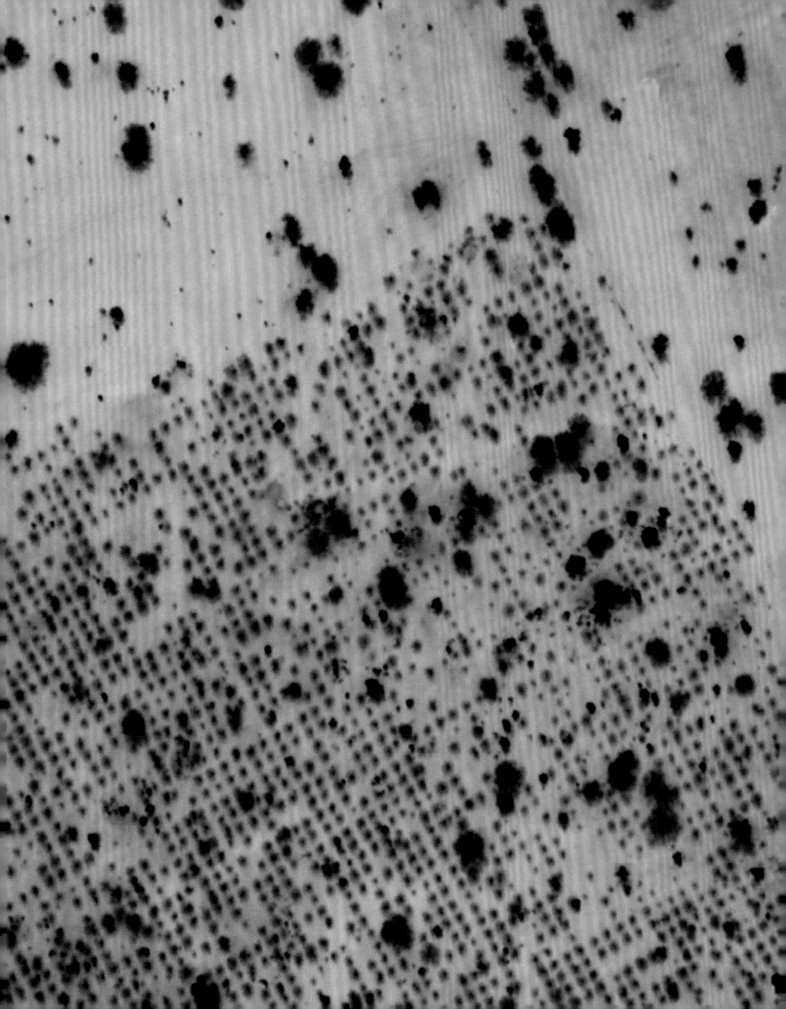

THE GREEN AROUND THE WALL

ROB LEVINTHAL

Rob Levinthal is a PhD candidate at the University of Pennsylvania with degrees in landscape architecture and environmental studies. He was a Peace Corps Volunteer from 2013–2015 in Senegal, where he served as an agroforestry extension agent. He returned to Africa in 2019 on a fellowship to research mega-infrastructure projects in Senegal and Ethiopia. Levinthal was a Landscape Architecture Foundation Olmsted Scholar Finalist in 2020.

✛ LANDSCAPE ARCHITECTURE, ECOLOGY

Senegal

Ethiopia

Ferlo

Long before the scramble for Africa and the Atlantic slave trade ravaged the continent, the Sahara Desert looked much different than the hellscape we know today. As recently as 8,000 years ago the Sahara was a landscape of sprawling grasslands, forests, and lakes. An emerging theory suggests that the tipping point in creating what is now the world's largest desert most likely came from anthropogenic causes – burning grassland to hunt and fend off predators, and grazing livestock for consumption.[1] Fast forward to the present day and the semi-arid region of the Sahel—the first productive ecosystem south of the Sahara—is threatened with a similar fate. This time anthropogenic causes, both in the region and abroad, are increasing the desert's range by roughly 10% in the last century into parts of the Sahel.[2] Despite even harsher conditions expected in the area in the coming years, international hope in restoring the landscape persists in the form of the so-called Great Green Wall (pictured on previous page). Founded in 2007 by the African Union and funded by the United Nations, World Bank, and European Union, this multibillion-dollar initiative strives to keep the Sahelian landscape green and stymie the exodus of climate refugees at the Sahel's northern border. However, belief in this project as a panacea in its current form underestimates the forces shaping the region. If the Sahel is to avoid runaway land degradation it will need more than a green wall.

Stretching across the entire breadth of the African continent from Senegal to Eritrea, the Sahel is mostly flat and may resemble what the Sahara once looked like, although without the large bodies of water. Rainfall ranges from 6 to 27.5 inches per year.[3] Droughts are commonplace and have been known to significantly vary in length and intensity. Records show that a megadrought existed over the entire region for several centuries (1400–1750);[4] more recently a drought lasted several decades (from the 1970s–1980s) over the western half of the Sahel, from which the rainfall has never fully recovered.[5] In the past decade, several year-long droughts (2010, 2012, 2018) threatened millions of the region's children with starvation.[6] The majority of predictive modeling shows this region continuing to dry and droughts becoming more prevalent.[7] However, some research conversely indicates that as the Mediterranean Sea warms, this semi-arid ecosystem could see more rainfall,[8] although it will likely be destructive in form.[9] Regardless, the Sahel represents one of the world's most vulnerable regions subject to human-induced climate change and represents the frontline of things to come.[10]

While the economically developed world attempts to curb its emissions and slow global warming to a 1.5–2°C increase in temperature this century, the Sahel's climate is projected to rise at a rate 1.5 times higher than the global average.[11] An increase of 6°C is considered a real possibility here, making much of the landscape uninhabitable in the hot season.[12] Even with a moderate increase in temperature, the production of corn and staple crops like sorghum and millet (used in nearly every meal) will significantly decline.[13] And, just as these crop yields are forecast to decrease, population growth in the region is surging. In 1950 there were slightly over 30 million people living in the Sahel. Today there are well over 125 million, and in the next 30 years the population is expected to reach 340 million.[14] Along with projected shortages of food and fresh water, these factors are contributing to political instability, with war, terrorism, and religious extremism gaining strong footholds in many countries in the Sahel. Furthermore, the inability to create a decent living or feed their families drives many (usually men) to flee the Sahelian landscape for neighboring cities (now megacities) or other countries in the hope of finding income to send remittances home. A good example of this exodus is occurring across the agro-silvopasture landscapes of the Ferlo in Senegal.

The Ferlo's History

Existing outside the productive land adjacent to the Atlantic coast and the arable floodplains of the Senegal River, the Ferlo is a large stretch of land with no naturally occurring bodies of water. Because of this, it has long withstood the pressures of extensive human intervention found elsewhere in Africa. In the early- to mid-1900s, the Ferlo was home to lions, giraffes, elephants, ostriches, and many of the other charismatic megafauna commonly associated with the African savanna.[15] Humans would only use this land in the rainy season when temporary pools of standing water existed in sandy depressions. During three waterlogged months from July to September, Fulani pastoral cattle herders migrated from the nearby floodplains to gorge their cattle on the Ferlo's plentiful grasses, and hunting camps were set up to capture game before having to return to more reliable freshwater sources.[16] Following the rainy season, the landscape was able to recover from the occupation of the herders' heavy-hooved cattle, creating a balanced environment.

In the 1950s, however, the Ferlo underwent a dramatic transformation. Still subject to colonial domination, the French built 51 boreholes throughout the Ferlo, using motors to pull water from the previously inaccessible aquifer and allowing more permanent occupation of the land. Following Senegal's independence in 1960, additional boreholes and their maintenance were funded by the United States and many other countries as a means of well-intended charity. As a result, cattle and small ruminants like sheep and goats have been widely introduced into this previously inaccessible landscape[17] with significant detrimental effects.[18] Huge swaths of bare soil are now exposed to the intense sun, and seedlings no longer reach the canopy due to the indomitable appetite of the goats. Displaced indigenous ungulates and the predators that once kept overgrazing in check have long been extirpated.[19]

The Ferlo's Present

Despite its natural precarity, it is here in the Ferlo that the majority of the Senegalese section of the Great Green Wall takes shape. While not a continuous green ribbon across the arid landscape as the project's name suggests, the wall exists rather as a patchwork of different interventions in a variable bandwidth of land deemed the most susceptible to desertification. In the summer of 2019 I visited some of these projects throughout the Ferlo and interviewed those involved. Guidance was provided by staff of the Great Green Wall,

Senegal's Eaux et Foret, and the UN's Food and Agriculture Organization from their base camps in Mbar Toubab and Widou Thiengoly.

All the greening projects around these basecamps—including one as large as 1,000 hectares—start with fencing to encourage natural regeneration without the presence of domesticated animals. Typically, within a few years, two-foot-tall golden grasses have recolonized the land and stand in stark contrast to the red sand and dung on the other side of the fence. Patches of land such as these then serve as important wildlife refuges for both migrating and local/endemic species.[20] In the largest project, kudus, gazelles, and tortoises have also been reintroduced inside the fences. Also a working habitat, some enclosures permit cattle to graze inside the grassed lot for a small fee during the driest time of the year. Highlighting the scarcity of grass found throughout the region, theft of this grass is a common problem. Serving as a grass bank, these areas can eventually be reforested by reseeding as cattle avoid eating tree saplings.

Whether from overgrazing or the shortening of the rainy season from three months to around three weeks since the droughts of the 1970s, tree diversity in the Ferlo has dwindled to just four dominant species. The basecamp Widou Thiengoly is the local name for a tree that was once abundant around the borehole town but is no longer found in the area. In response to this loss of biodiversity, two fenced 300-hectare lots were created to reintroduce 13 native species from the original Sahelian scrub. In these recreated landscapes the selected tree species favor those that can be utilized for food, gum, and traditional medicines, though native species with less human utility are not entirely absent. While the fences used here are only temporary and typically last for five years, they give the trees the necessary head start needed to survive the constant grazing.[21]

Women's gardens are another type of productive intervention. These gardens help fulfill the Great Green Wall's commitment to the UN's fifth Sustainable Development Goal to support gender equality by giving women more autonomy through financial independence and the ability to grow fruits and vegetables to improve the diets of their children.[22] Near a successful women's garden, is the Great Green Wall's newest intervention type run by a single family. This 100-hectare fenced lot is maintained by Djina Ka, who leads the local women's group sponsored by the Great Green Wall in Widou Thiengoly. In her family compound, like many compounds in the area, the adult men have left in search of better wages to support their extensive families. Two young boys under the age of 15 were thus tasked with patrolling this large lot for any intruders or wandering ruminants. For their service, their sheep are permitted to graze the enclosure before Tabaski (Eid al-Adha), fattening them for sale at the market for religious sacrifice.

1 David K. Wright, "Humans as Agents in the Termination of the African Humid Period," *Frontiers in Earth Science* 5 (2017).

2 Natalie Thomas & Sumant Nigam, "Twentieth-Century Climate Change over Africa: Seasonal hydroclimate Trends and Sahara Desert Expansion," *Journal of Climate* 31, no. 9 (2018): 3349–70.

3 Rasmus Fensholt, et al., "Assessing Land Degradation/Recovery in the African Sahel from Long-Term Earth Observation Based Primary Productivity and Precipitation Relationships," *Remote Sensing* 5 (2013): 664–86.

4 Catherine Brahic, "Africa Trapped in Mega-drought Cycle," *New Scientist* (April 16, 2009), https://www.newscientist.com/article/dn16967-africa-trapped-in-mega-drought-cycle/.

5 Hanne Kristine Adriansen, "Livelihood Dynamics of Pastoralists in Ferlo, Senegal," *Proceedings of the 15th Danish Sahel Workshop* 15 (2013): 179–201.

6 Nellie Peyton, "U.N Calls for Urgent aid to Sahel as Hunger Crisis Loom," *Reuters* (May 3, 2018), https://www.reuters.com/article/us-sahel-hunger-un/u-n-calls-for-urgent-aid-to-sahel-as-hunger-crisis-looms-idUSKBN1I42CL.

7 Ove D. Hoegh-Guldberg, et al., "Impacts of 1.5°C Global Warming on Natural and Human Systems," in *Global Warming of 1.5°C. An IPCC Special Report* (2018).

8 Jong-yeon Park, Jurgen Bader & Daniela Matei. "Anthropogenic Mediterranean Warming Essential Driver for Present and Future Sahel Rainfall," *Nature Climate Change* 6 (2016): 941–45.

9 Hoegh-Guldberg, et al., "Impacts of 1.5°C Global Warming on Natural and Human Systems."

10 Lyse Doucet, "The Battle on the Frontline of Climate Change in Mali," *BBC News* (January 22, 2019), https://www.bbc.com/news/the-reporters-46921487 (Accessed on August 18, 2020).

11 Joe Penney, "West Africa's Sahel Region is Especially Vulnerable to Climate Change but also Weak Governance," *Quartz Africa* (October 1, 2019), https://qz.com/africa/1719442/west-africas-sahel-vulnerable-to-climate-change-bad-governance/.

12 Ibid.

13 Hoegh-Guldberg, et al., "Impacts of 1.5°C Global Warming on Natural and Human Systems."

14 Malcolm Potts, et al., "Crisis in the Sahel: Possible Solutions and Consequences of Inaction," *The Oasis Initiative* (2013).

15 Henri Barrall, "Le Ferlo des Forages: Gestion Ancienne et Actuelle de L'espace Pastoral," *ORSTOM* (1982).

16 Hanne Kirstine Adriansen & Thomas Theis Nielsen, "Going Where the Grass is Greener: On the Study of Pastoral Mobility in Ferlo, Senegal," *Human Ecology* 30, 2 (2002): 215–26.

Left: A herder's fenced compound at the Great Green Wall in Senegal's Ferlo.

17 Morgane Dendoncker, Douda Ngom & Caroline Vincke, "Tree Dynamics (1955–2012) and their Uses in the Senegal's Ferlo Region: Insights from a Historical Vegetation Database, Local Knowledge and Field Inventories," *Bois et Forets des Tropiques*, 326 no. 4 (2015): 25–41.

18 Leo Zwarts, Rob G. Bijlsma & Jan van der Kamp, "Large Decline of Birds in Sahelian Rangeland due to Loss of Woody Cover and Soil Seed Bank," *Journal of Arid Environments* 155 (2018): 1–15.

19 Hanne Kirstine Adriansen & Thomas Theis Nielsen, "Going Where the Grass is Greener: On the Study of Pastoral Mobility in Ferlo, Senegal," *Human Ecology* 30 no. 2 (2002): 215–26.

20 Zwarts et al., "Large Decline of Birds in Sahelian Rangeland due to Loss of Woody Cover and Soil Seed Bank," 1–15.

21 Mignane Sarr, Food and Agriculture Organization, Interview with author.

22 IISD/SDG Knowledge Hub, "A Green Wall of Hope for Africa"(May 2, 2016), http://sdg. iisd.org/commentary/guest-articles/a-green-wall-of-hope-for-africa/.

23 Lars Laestadius, "Africa has Plans for a Great Green Wall: Why the Idea needs a Rethink," *The Conversation* (June 18, 2017), https://theconversation.com/africas-got-plans-for-a-great-green-wall-why-the-idea-needs-a-rethink-78627.

24 Richard Escadefal, et al., "The African Great Green Wall Project: What Advice can Scientists Provide?" *French Scientific Committee on Desertification*, http://www.csf-desertification.eu/combating-desertification/item/the-african-great-green-wall-project (Accessed July 28, 2020).

25 Colleen Moser, "It Takes a Village: Despite Challenges, Migrant Groups Lead Development in Senegal," *Migration Policy Institute* (October 4, 2018), https://www.migrationpolicy.org/article/it-takes-village-despite-challenges-migrant-groups-lead-development-senegal.

26 National Public Radio: All Things Considered, "Why the Villages are Losing their Young Men," https://www.npr.org/sections/goatsandsoda/2016/05/05/474972869/why-the-villages-are-losing-their-young-men.

27 S. Mulitza, et al., "Increase in African dust flux at the onset of commercial agriculture in the Sahel region," *Nature* 466 (2010): 226–28.

28 W. M. Adams, "Wasting the Rain: Rivers, People and Planning in Africa" (University of Minnesota Press, 1992).

29 Mabel Gundlach, "Saving the Soil in Senegal's Peanut Basin," *DW* (short film).

30 Nathan McClintock & Amadou Makhtar Diop, "Soil Fertility Management and Compost Use in Senegal's Peanut Basin," *International Journal of Agricultural Sustainability* 3, no. 2 (2004): 79–91.

Opposite: Church forests in Ethiopia protect the remnant native vegetation.

There is no denying that the Great Green Wall in the Ferlo has made an enormous impact on communities in the susceptible northern edge of the Sahel, enhancing lives like those of Djina Ka and her family. Yet the Sahel in Senegal is much wider than the line of built and proposed interventions drawn across the Ferlo and is wider still than Richard St. Barbe Baker's original 1952 vision of a 50-km-wide greenbelt of trees across the continent from which the idea of the Great Green Wall originates.[23] Contrary to common belief, desertification does not just happen at the edge of the desert and its neighboring ecosystem, but throughout that entire vulnerable ecosystem as it is exposed to climate change and human activity. While ruminants put extreme pressure on the Ferlo, this land also represents some of the least populated in Senegal, and its recent past begs the question whether permanent occupation was sustainable in the first place.

Population density is much greater in the floodplains of the Senegal River,[24] the Tambacounda region,[25] and throughout the Peanut Basin,[26] regions all exhibiting similar emigration patterns. The latter, aptly named for its production of groundnuts, receives just enough rainfall to practice a single season of rain-fed agriculture each year. Over a century of peanut monoculture (with colonial and state pressure to cut down trees and use unsustainable agricultural technologies)[27] has put a strain on the environment comparable to the semi-sedentary pastoralism of the Ferlo.[28] In the Peanut Basin, clearing of forest and scrub for cultivated land persists[29] and is rapidly expanding in the Tambacounda region and throughout all of the arable western Sahel.[30] Furthermore, the pressures of rapid population growth cause the land to be more intensely cultivated as it gets divided among the growing families. Cropland loss due to soil exhaustion in the Peanut Basin is now becoming common with large areas left to fallow, leading to further population displacement.[31] Thus, if the Sahelian landscape is to be saved and high emigration rates are to be reduced, a secondary defense against widespread land degradation must be implemented in the Sahelian interior as well.

A Secondary Defense – a Web not a Wall

Top-down mega-infrastructure aimed at addressing large-scale land degradation has been successful in attracting global attention, but the projects are often flawed in their scope and on-the-ground practices. In the service of the Great Green Wall project, for example, thousands of trees have been planted and lost because of the desire to create a literal wall across the continent, sometimes in places where trees have never existed.[32] The Great Green Wall vision was based on an outdated definition of desertification and understanding of land degradation, which does not only occur at the desert's edge but also in densely populated semi-arid areas where human activity is great.[33] What is therefore needed is a

secondary defense to protect a greater number of people from the effects of land degradation throughout the Sahel and not just at the ecosystem's northernmost edge. While large, fenced lots may be the best solution in the pastoral areas like the Ferlo, prolific small-scale approaches based on the needs of local communities are necessary in the agricultural regions. One potential community-driven intervention that could be emulated here is Ethiopia's church forests.

Ethiopia does not exist within the natural boundaries of the semi-arid Sahel, but because of its degraded landscape, rampant deforestation, and exploding population, it has been included in the Great Green Wall. In the early decades of the 20th century nearly half of the country was covered by Afromontane forest. Today just 5% remains. Most of this old growth forest is found within the 35,000 Ethiopian Orthodox Church grounds in the northern half of the country.[34] These churches consider the surrounding area to be holy land and so deforestation has been slow nearby. The NGO Tree Foundation and community efforts led by locals, such as Abebaw Atinkut's Korata Kebele Reforestation Project, which I visited in 2019 and 2020, are actively working to build fences to protect these church forests from further encroachment of farms and ruminants. In agriculture, Trees for the Future, One Acre Fund, and numerous other NGOs are using agroforestry and garden forests to help produce more food sustainably on less land while working amicably within these communities. Despite this dynamic work, foreign investment in building fences for other greening initiatives at sacred and secular institutions in villages are sites of untapped potential across the entire region. Funding and designing what these sites may look like in other countries could ignite a new wave of environmental revitalization and activism rooted in local practices.

Trees throughout Senegal, like the Ethiopian church forests, primarily survive when protected against ruminants. Of the 4,000 trees that my work partners and I planted during my time as an Agroforestry Extension Agent with the Peace Corps in Senegal (2013–2015), roughly 80% of the 1,200 that survived had some sort of protection. In most cases this included metal or concrete fences, "sakket" (fences made of intertwined straw), thorny branches tied around saplings, tree guards, or live fences of native thorny species. Fences are also found around community institutions though they are not intended for environmental restoration purposes. Similarly, they are important infrastructure seen throughout villages as it is an Islamic custom to enclose family compounds.[35]

Drame Sadiabou, the village of roughly 600 subsistence farmers in which I lived, had fences around the dahra (Islamic school) and elementary school, which were funded and built by the community with remittances sent home from family members abroad. While the central mosque's enclosure in the village was built in 2015, the second mosque in the village still aspires to build its own. The women's garden's fence was financed by the USAID/Peace Corps in 2011, and neighboring village garden plots managed by men are protected with live fences. An opportunity presents itself here with these desired and existing fences. With outside funding, fences around schools and dahras can be expanded and used to plant and protect a greater number of trees to help educate students about the role and importance of a healthy environment. At mosques, fruit trees can also provide food for the needy during the "hungry season," and the proliferation of built women's gardens can be intercropped with trees to provide shade for vegetables and community gatherings.

Aside from the persistent bush and the few ancient baobabs, kola, and kapok trees sprinkled throughout the fields too large to fell, a small patch of forest without fences exists at the edge of every village. These forests are the last vestiges of native vegetation at the southern border of the Sahel in Senegal and uniquely house the village cemeteries. Here the dead are laid to rest in a small grove of naturally occurring floral species. Few fences guard the graveyard, though they are desired. No slash-and-burn of organic material takes place here, and ruminants are actively discouraged from grazing by the heckling of children and adults. In response, native species flourish, groundcover of leaves and insects abound, birds flock, and flowers and mushrooms seen nowhere else in the region grow. These cemeteries, despite their humble size, are reminiscent of the much larger church forests in Ethiopia. They should be expanded, reforested, and made into similar spaces of contemplation and respite. Creating protected areas in sacred and secular institutions with greening initiatives, coupled with an effort to make corridors of agroforestry in the fields between them, can create a second web of defense stronger than a wall to protect against land degradation in the Sahelian interior.

Conclusion

The people in the Sahel produce only 3% of the world's greenhouse gas emissions.[36] Many live without electricity or running water, let alone cars, air travel, or air conditioning, and yet they bear the biggest brunt of the effects of a changing climate. The UN acknowledged this injustice when helping fund the Paris Agreement, which pledged $25 billion over five years starting in 2020 to low- and moderate-income countries disproportionately affected by climate change. However, this initiative is being defunded and dismantled by far-right politicians.[37] The Sahel is at the frontline of climate change, yet further funding for projects like the Great Green Wall is uncertain. Failing to produce a secondary defense in the Sahelian interior will force an even greater exodus of its current population, and cause the loss of millions of hectares of arable land to desert. While large-scale interventions need to be recommitted to and expanded in pastoral areas, a plethora of small-scale interventions in agricultural zones has the potential to produce the positive environmental impact needed across the entire interior where large-scale projects are unsuitable. Global top-down initiatives such as the Great Green Wall can provide powerful images for public buy-in and funding, but local conditions present obstacles rendering many of these ideas invalid. While the notion of a wall of trees standing firm against a sea of sand is provocative and certainly helps create interest, projects must reflect the realities of local communities and their daily lives. By investing in greening opportunities in existing and proposed Sahelian schools, places of worship, cemeteries, and women's gardens, and connecting them with corridors of intercropped trees, there is a real chance to combat some of the detrimental effects of human-induced climate change.

31 USAID & USGS, "Agricultural Expansion Across West Africa," https://eros.usgs.gov/westafrica/agriculture-expansion [Accessed July 26, 2020].

32 David O'Connor & James Ford, "Increasing the Effectiveness of the Great Green Wall as an Adaptation to the Effects of Climate Change and Desertification," *Sustainability* 6, no. 10 (2014): 7142–514.

33 Adams, "Wasting the Rain: Rivers, People and Planning in Africa."

34 Alison Abbott, "Biodiversity Thrives in Ethiopia's Church Forests," *Nature*, https://www.nature.com/immersive/d41586-019-00275-x/index.html [Accessed August 21, 2020].

35 Ambe J. Njoh, "Planning Power: Town Planning and Social Control in Colonial Africa" (University College London Press, 2007).

36 Penney, "West Africa's Sahel Region is Especially Vulnerable to Climate Change but also Weak Governance."

37 Matthew Lockwood, "Right-Wing Populism and Climate Change Policy," Oxford Research Group (June 13, 2019), https://www.oxfordresearchgroup.org.uk/blog/right-wing-populism-and-climate-change-policy.

GREEN STUFF

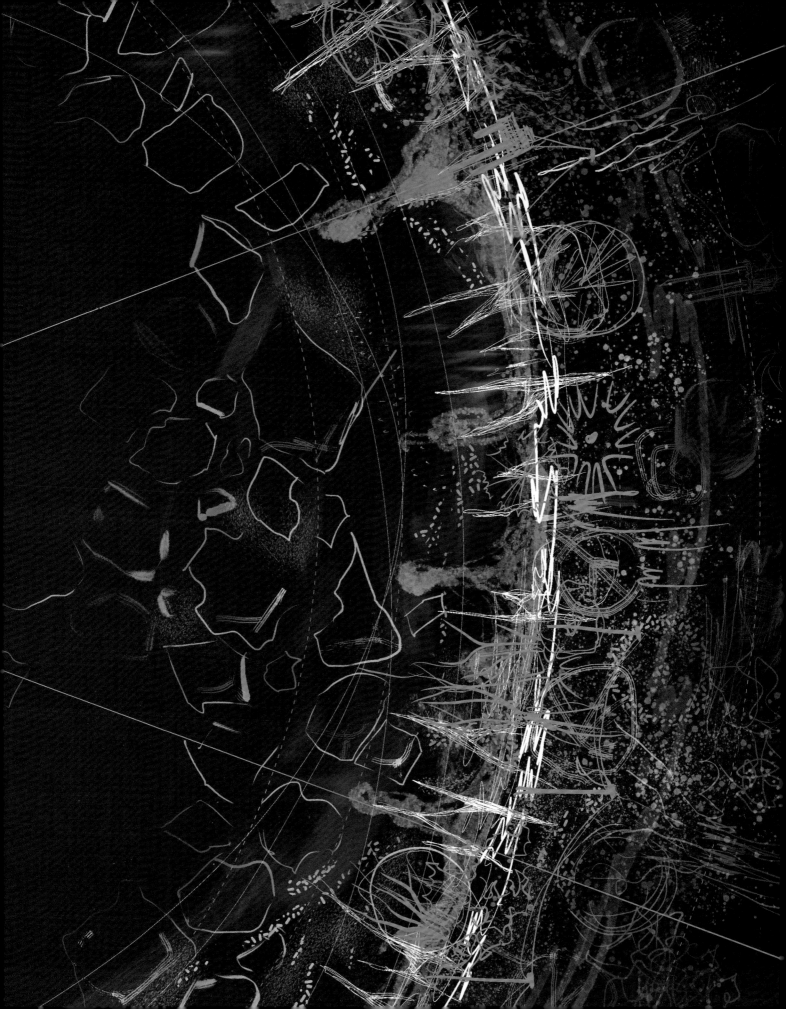

RICHARD WELLER

Richard Weller is professor and chair of landscape architecture at the University of Pennsylvania where he also holds the Meyerson Chair of Urbanism. He is author of a number of books including *Boomtown 2050: Scenarios for a Rapidly Growing City* (2009), *Made in Australia: The Future of Australian Cities* (2014), and *Beautiful China: Reflections on Landscape Architecture in Contemporary China* (2020). Weller's recent research on global flashpoints between urbanism and biodiversity has been published in *National Geographic* and *Scientific American*, while the related design work was exhibited at the Venice Biennale of Architecture (2021).

✛ ART, DESIGN

Describing his recent exhibition *Critical Zones* concerning the future of life on earth, the philosopher Bruno Latour wrote, "We have done our best to reject the use of any balloon form, any pumpkin-sized Mother Earth, any Blue Planet, or any green stuff."[1] I presume by "green stuff" he means plants. Latour would have nothing against plants per se, but he would certainly take issue with the way in which they are used as surrogates for that thing called "nature," especially when it is positioned as something different to and separate from culture. Reinforcing this difference and separation is exactly what happens every time someone says something like "we need more nature in the city," when what they really mean is more "green stuff." Indeed, landscape architects and ecologists—who really should know better—often say this kind of thing. To be fair, it's easy to do – it's just an innocent convention.

But invoking such a momentous word as "nature," is never innocent – especially not for those whose professions claim it and our relations to it as their primary subject matter. Most famously, for example, in his manifesto *Design with Nature* Ian McHarg drew on the word nature to bolster what was essentially a practical concern with appropriate land use and expand it into a meta-theory of evolution and planetary salvation. "Design with Landscape," which is what his method really meant, just doesn't have the same kind of gravitas. Nature provides a certain cachet for the landscape architects and scientists who claim to represent it. But the price of invoking it is to write oneself into an untenable contradiction – for as much as one might intend to merge nature and culture into new forms of endosymbiosis, its invocation reinforces the very opposite: dualism.[2]

I've been teaching a history-theory class called "The Culture of Nature" centered on this long-running problem in western thought for the last 25 years or so. Each year, the very first thing I ask the class to do is write down their answer to the question "What is nature?" I give them three minutes to respond. After class, I type the answers into a single document and circulate it to the class so that everyone can reflect on what is, for all intents and purposes, a multi-brained snapshot of what we collectively think the world, aka nature, is. I am often moved by the poetic and philosophical nuances of the answers – joy in some and melancholy in others. But so, too, each year I am amazed by the way in which, for a small but not insignificant minority, the belief that nature is not human-made or artificial persists. In a word, dualism.

Most of the answers fall somewhere within the range of John Stuart Mill's 1874 fourfold definition of nature as (1) everything,

(2) not culture, (3) things as they ought to be, and (4) the mysterious potential of things.[3] Each year there will be quite a few cosmological 1s; a defiant minority of 2s; a bunch of preachy environmentalist 3s, and a very small number of tentative and thoughtful 4s. Among the many inferences one could draw from this annual thought experiment, the main thing I've noticed over the years is that there has been an increase in answers falling into a fifth category that Mill, for whatever reason, did not feel necessary to include, namely that before it is anything else, nature is a cultural construct. For students with a Western liberal arts education the cultural construct caveat is now more or less the norm. And yet, having declared it as such, they will nonetheless typically proceed with their next few sentences to write themselves back within range of Mill's original four categories. Notably, only two students—out of what must be more than 800 by now—have ever taken the caveat to its logical conclusion and responded that "it's just a word." And no one has ever channeled Socrates to declare that the question is a trick and that there can be no answer because we just don't know, and for that matter, can probably never know. For my part, I come clean that I think "it's just a word" and "we don't know" are, in fact, the correct answers. And with that out of the way, we drop down just before the agricultural revolution and head for the Anthropocene.

Since the meme of the Anthropocene is defined as not just a concept but a planetary material phenomenon, there is, I think, now a sixth category of nature to which we must also turn our attention – terrestrial nature as a material work in progress. "What is nature?" now becomes "What is the nature of the Anthropocene (or Capitalocene,[4] if you prefer) that we have made and are making and what is our role as makers within it?" To summarily consider this in the space of a short article I propose to visit four major exhibitions that neatly span the same timeframe in which I have been conducting my experiment with the students. We begin with *Artificial Nature* curated by Jeffrey Deitch at the Deste Foundation for Contemporary Art in Athens in 1990[5] and then jump to two major shows which both took place in 2019: *Broken Nature* held at the XXIII Triennale di Milano (and later MoMA in New York) curated by Paolo Antonelli and Ala Tannir,[6] and *Nature: Cooper Hewitt Design Triennial* curated by Andrea Lipps, Matilda McQuaid, Caitlin Condell, and Gene Bertrand for the Cooper Hewitt Smithsonian Design Museum in New York.[7] The fourth exhibition we will visit is *Critical Zones: The Science and Politics of Landing on Earth* curated by Bruno Latour and Peter Weibel at the Center for Art and Media in Karlsruhe, Germany in 2020.[8] In these four similarly themed exhibitions and their associated publications—enough I think to constitute a movement of sorts—a large cast of contemporary artists, designers, scientists, historians, and philosophers have been brought together to critically appraise the nature of the Anthropocene and our role within it.[9]

In 1990 when Jeffrey Deitch launched the exhibition *Artificial Nature*, several significant things were in the air. The memory of the 1986 Chernobyl disaster was still vivid, Bill McKibben had just declared "the end of nature" as we knew it,[10] and Donna Haraway's formulation of the cyborg (wherein the boundaries between humans, animals, and machines were dissolving) was gaining notoriety.[11] Additionally, it was in that same year that Tim Berners-Lee effectively founded the internet with the invention of multi-nodal hypertext, and the first 3-D digital games were launched on the open market. It is no mistake then that a sense of being on the cusp of major technological, environmental, and philosophical change finds its way not only into the *Artificial Nature* exhibition, but especially into its subsequent book.

In the book, Deitch, in collaboration with Dan Friedman, presents a raucous, postmodern visual essay. They sample first-generation digital imagery, old film stills, advertising clichés and artworks ranging from Poussin to Koons, all of which are emblazoned with large provocative statements. For example, over a close-up of a group of Barbie dolls is written "Nature is less the mysterious nourishing force that emerged with the birth of the universe and more and more something that we are re-creating ourselves."[12] Text over a photograph of a 1950s model in a bikini holding a watering can to plastic flowers reads "Whatever happens, for better or for worse, nature as our ancestors knew it may soon be finished,"[13] and set over an image of a person in a hospital hooked up to a ventilator is: "The environment has become so artificial that the traditional aspiration of the artist to 'reveal the truth' in what he or she sees may have become impossible."[14] And so it goes. Every page is a visual and verbal punchline until it ends with an unfiltered image of what appears to be a perfectly "natural" waterfall, whereupon they hammer in their final nail: "Genuine nature may now be more artificial than natural."[15] The end.

Artificial Nature unflinchingly grasped the zeitgeist of the late 1980s and set the aesthetic sensibility for how artists would engage with the otherwise romantic subject of nature thereafter. What is stunning from today's perspective is not the overtly grotesque aesthetics of artificiality that it lauded, but that climate change was never even mentioned. In the two blockbuster exhibitions of 2019–*Broken Nature* and *Nature: Cooper Hewitt Design Triennial*–climate change permeates everything. The second major point of difference between

these exhibitions is that while *Artificial Nature* was primarily concerned with the end of nature's representation, the 2019 shows are primarily about how both artists and designers are actively seeking restorative agency within it.

In *Broken Nature* Antonelli's curatorial position and intent is unambiguous: "We have managed to raise Earth's temperature... We have deforested, drilled, mined, fertilized and sterilized, extracted, removed mountaintops, and terraformed our own planet—and intend to do it to others. Design is a powerful analysis and repair tool. Designers should teach the world how they can be used well...design can help by acting as a cognitive, pragmatic, and political tool. It can be restorative."[16] Similarly, in the Cooper Hewitt show the curators explain that "the designers in this publication and exhibition understand that we must enlist nature as a guide and partner to alter the imbalance of human impact on our world. The approach is transdisciplinary and involves scientists, engineers, advocates for social and environmental justice, artists, and philosophers who apply their conjoined knowledge toward a more harmonious and regenerative future."[17]

As evidenced by over 150 works across both of the 2019 shows this movement is not about the proliferation of ever more attractively designed products, it is, according to Antonelli, design as a "cooperation with other protagonists...from bacteria to silkworms and plants – and even minerals." It is "to think of designing systems, networks, and families rather than discrete objects...to be inspired by the efficiencies and sensitivities of other species' social structures and infrastructures."[18] Design, Antonelli concludes, "should be centered not only on humans but on the future of the whole biosphere as well."[19] Examples of this include rubber fiber that mimics coral, adhesives derived from slugs, sports shoes fashioned from ocean plastics, car exhaust condensed into ink, bacteria used to dye clothes and grow bricks, screws made of silk, self-composting burials, digital recreations of extinct species, shoes that sow seeds, furniture manufactured from e-waste, food made from human cell tissue, tableware created from food waste, lichen facades, and so on.

The inventiveness of all this prototyping is by any measure remarkable, but as ever with trends in design culture some of it also risks being a bit too cool for its own good. On the one hand, in the same way nanobots might repair tissue from within the body as opposed to the old-school approach of amputating an entire limb, the admixture of technology, novel materials, and living systems in this work represents a new level of ingenuity and sophistication for design intelligence. On the other hand, some of the work fetishizes bio-tech and is only tenuously linked to the trinity of science, social justice, and empathy for the nonhuman as is *de rigueur* in both triennial exhibitions and across the humanities more generally.

As the more critically reflexive artists in the shows manage to also broach in their otherwise optimistic work, it is a naive faith in technology and the veneration of incessant innovation at any cost that is what got us into the climate crisis in the first place. The curators, of course, know this: the introduction to the Cooper Hewitt exhibition, for example, ends with the disclaimer that the show also "probes and pokes at a techno-utopianism to remind us that in the end, design is not a panacea."[20] Truth be told, for both of these shows it actually is, and in a time of despair it is their optimistic inventiveness and at least their theoretical turn to and concern for the lifecycle and relationality of all things, that makes them so compelling.

To move deeper into the tension between despair and optimism, as well as questions of technology, science, ecology, human identity, and politics in the Anthropocene, we could do no better than (vicariously) visit *Critical Zones: The Science and Politics of Landing on Earth* curated by French philosopher Bruno Latour and Austrian artist Peter Weibel. Effectively invented and explored as an integrated whole by Alexander von Humboldt in the 19th century and further articulated by Vladimir Vernadsky, James Lovelock, and Lynn Margulis in the 20th century, the critical zone is a scientific term referring to the planetary skein of life between rock below and sky above. In other words, the critical zone is what would otherwise be called the biosphere and its study concerns its self-regulation and regeneration in relation to the lithosphere, hydrosphere, and atmosphere, which it in turn produces and is produced by. Today the scientific project of understanding these interactions is in part monitored through 45 worldwide Critical Zone Observatories where customized sensors at field stations collect data for specific research questions and are networked together into a scholarly whole that aims to create knowledge of the integrated earth system that is greater than merely the sum of its parts.

More than nature, in its conception the critical zone is also a technosphere: not only a scientific sensory apparatus, but a cultural landscape manipulated, not to say designed, by over 7.5 billion humans. The modern history of this is dominated by the fact that (some) humans have violently colonized and exploited the zone not so as to honor its awesome beauty and respectfully find their niche within it, but to exploit its riches, oppress its indigenous peoples, and in vain try to escape its

1 Bruno Latour, "Seven Objections against Landing on Earth" in Bruno Latour & Peter Weibel (eds), *Critical Zones: The Science and Politics of Landing on Earth* (The Center for Art and Media & MIT Press, 2020), 14.

2 It is worth noting that in the decades since McHarg wrote *Design With Nature* under the influence of the old paradigm of ecology (which treated humans and our institutions, built environment, and technology as inherently *external* to true ecological systems), the rise of *urban ecology* within the ecological disciplines has moved towards a more integrated model of nature and culture and embraced the "human ecosystem framework" (ie., socio-ecological systems) as the overarching paradigm for understanding the world. See Steward Pickett, et al., "Urban Ecological Systems: Linking Terrestrial, Ecological, Physical, and Socioeconomic Components of Metropolitan Areas" *Annual Review of Ecology and Systematics* 32 (2001): 127–57.

3 John Stuart Mill, "On Nature" in *Nature, The Utility of Religion and Theism* (Longmans, Green, Reader, and Dyer, 1874).

4 Jason W. Moore, *Anthropocene or Capitalocene? Nature, History, and the Crisis of Capitalism* (PM Press/Kairos, 2016).

5 Jeffrey Deitch & Dan Friedman (eds), *Artificial Nature* (Deste Foundation for Contemporary Art, 1990).

6 Paolo Antonelli & Ala Tannir (eds), *Broken Nature: XXIII Trienalle di Milano* (Rizzoli, 2019).

7 Andrea Lipps, et al. (eds), *Nature: Collaborations in Design* (Cooper Hewitt, Smithsonian Design Museum, 2019).

8 Bruno Latour & Peter Weibel (eds), *Critical Zones: The Science and Politics of Landing on Earth* (The Center for Art and Media & MIT Press, 2020).

9 Adding to the sense that recent exhibitions focusing on new constructs of nature amount to a movement, see also Designs for Different Futures curated by Kathryn B. Hiesinger and Michelle Millar Fisher at the Philadelphia Museum of Art. Although it is not solely about new constructs of nature, Designs for Different Futures does feature artists and also focus in part on very similar issues facing design culture in the Anthropocene, see, Kathryn B. Hiesinger (ed.), *Designs for Different Futures* (Yale University Press, 2019).

10 Bill McKibben, *The End of Nature* (Random House, 1989).

11 The Cyborg Manifesto was first published in in 1985; See Donna Haraway, "Manifesto for Cyborgs: Science, Technology, and Socialist Feminism in the 1980s," *Socialist Review* 80 (1985): 65–108, and then again in 1991 in Haraway's hugely influential book *Simians, Cyborgs and Women: The Reinvention of Nature* (Routledge, 1981).

earthly limitations (gravity, bodies, entropy, resources, etc.). The entire creative project of the *Critical Zones* exhibition and eponymous book then revolves around the metaphor of how to end this Faustian hallucination and return to earth. This is not a return to Mother Nature, or any other historical nature, but instead a new discovery of how the earth works and how we might "land" within it. Put succinctly, the *Critical Zones* exhibition is about turning religion and modernity upside down and circumscribing a new earthly cosmology.

Bringing the arts and the sciences together, as the exhibition does, is then a profoundly ambitious and yet necessarily modest, experimental beginning for creating new words, images, maps, data, and assemblages that flesh out this new cosmology. As explored in the exhibition and book, the aim is not only to land on this new earth but most importantly to avoid crash landing. According to the array of scientific and artistic material gathered for the show, the way to do this is through forensic attention to the ecological and cultural details of particular places as opposed to global views from nowhere such as GIS mapping or incantations at the altar of the Blue Marble. Going by the available evidence, however, it seems that once Latour's "earthlings" have made their landing they (perhaps intentionally) don't seem to have a plan for what will happen next.

The people whose job it is to make earthly plans are landscape architects. Remarkably, however, of the hundreds of designers in all four exhibitions only one landscape architect is featured.[21] Despite landscape architecture being a field of endeavor that actively creates new hybrids of culture, technology, and ecology, and despite it having considerable influence over sizeable tracts of the critical zone and being, at least in principle, philosophically aligned with the curatorial agendas behind these shows, it is completely ignored.

Why is this? Perhaps the work we do is perceived as only smearing reactionary "green stuff" over issues with roots so deep that only philosophers and artists can get to them. Perhaps the green stuff we work with carries too much reactionary and aristocratic baggage, or, perhaps, because green stuff is paradisiacal and not utopian it is considered ahistorical and unworthy of inclusion in discourse. Or maybe we are simply overlooked because we don't conduct and couch our practices as experimental, critical, and innovative in the way other participants in these shows do. Perhaps we are not working closely enough with both scientists and artists. Perhaps the contradictions between our own long-standing commitment to "landing" and the fact that the profession is generally beholden to commercial development disqualifies it outright. Perhaps we are just too busy making plans to think about any of this.

It is particularly ironic that at the same time that these major exhibitions were occurring landscape architecture was also staging its own blockbuster focused on the very same themes of design and nature as the others. The *Design with Nature Now* exhibition held at the University of Pennsylvania to commemorate the 50th anniversary of Ian McHarg's manifesto *Design With Nature* showcased 25 design projects that, according to the curators, offer "real clues as to how, through design, we can better tune our cities and their infrastructure to the forces and flows of the Earth system."[22] Although one can only wonder whether the philosophers would approve of them, projects such as the ecological restoration of the Fresh Kills landfill in New York, the Great Green Wall through the African Sahel, the greening of the Ruhr region's postindustrial sites in Germany, the Sand Motor on the coast of Holland, and the Yellowstone to Yukon (Y2Y) conservation corridor in North America would seem to manifest in powerful and topical ways the issues and aspirations highlighted across all the exhibitions we have visited. These projects are signs of historical change in how humans treat the earth and inscribe themselves into it: how they might not just design *with* nature–as if it were still some other thing–but design *within* it. And this "within" does not mean that we are imprisoned in the earth, for organisms make their environment just as they are simultaneously made by it, and whilst within this process there is ruthless constraint, so too there is creativity.

For the next big exhibition about how we understand and appreciate our situation as interpreters and creators of the world it would be good if philosophers, artists, historians, designers, *and* landscape architects came together. Perhaps we could call it "Green Stuff," which, after all, is the perfect model for how to exist in and cocreate the critical zone.

12 Deitch & Friedman, *Artificial Nature*, 12.

13 Ibid., 58.

14 Ibid., 86.

15 Ibid., 151.

16 Paola Antonelli, "Broken Nature" in Antonelli & Tannir (eds), *Broken Nature*, 18–21.

17 Lipps, et al. (eds), *Nature: Collaborations in Design*, 6.

18 Antonelli, "Broken Nature" in Antonelli & Tannir (eds), *Broken Nature*, 27.

19 Ibid., 40.

20 Lipps, et al. (eds), *Nature: Collaborations in Design*, 14.

21 That is, Anuradha Mathur, whose joint art- and theory-based design work with partner Dilip Da Cunha is included in *Critical Zones*.

22 Frederick Steiner, Richard Weller, Karen M'Closkey & Billy Fleming, *Design with Nature Now* (Lincoln Institute of Land Policy, 2019).

IMAGE CREDITS

Endpapers

The Hungry Lion Throws Itself on the Antelope (1905) by Henri Rousseau, public domain.

Editorial

p. 4: *Green* (2020) by Georg Bautz, used with permission.

The Color of Yearning

p. 6: *Embroidery Woman* (1817) by Georg Friedrich Kersting, public domain.

p. 9: *Napoleon in Vines* (2021) by Samuel Ridge, used with permission.

Green Screens in Eight Channels

p. 10: Image by Samuel Ridge (2021), used with permission.

p. 12: Still from *Cambio* (2020) by Formafantasma, used with permission via author.

p. 13: Still from *Dislocation Mystérieuse* (1901) by Georges Méliès, public domain.

p. 14: Samples from the Chicago Film Society's "Leader Ladies" Project (2011), courtesy of the Chicago Film Society, used with permission via author.

p. 15: *The Visible Invisible* (2018) by Stephanie Syjuco used with permission via author.

p. 16: Installation view of *Pavillion de L'Esprit Nouveau* (2015) at Swiss Institute. Photo by Daniel Perez, courtesy of Swiss Institute, used with permission via author.

p. 17: Installation view of *Remains in Development* (2020) by Felicity Hammond at C/O Berlin. Photo by David von Becker, used with permission via author.

p. 18: Installation view of *Screen Green* (2015–16) by Ho Rui An at "Public Spirits" (2016–17) at Centrum Sztuki Współczesnej Zamek Ujazdowski, Warsaw, Poland. Photo by Bartosz Górka, courtesy of Ho Rui An, used with permission via author.

p. 19: "Exterior Changi Airport Terminal 4, Singapore," author unknown, used under CC BY SA 4.0 license via Wikimedia Commons.

Trending Green: Landscape in The Age of Digital Reproduction

p. 20: Image by Leslie Jingyu Zhang (2021), incorporating "Brittlebush (Encelia farinosa) and unknown white wild flower, Death Valley Super Bloom" (2016) by Adorabutton, public domain (cropped & altered).

p. 24: Image by Parker Sutton (2020), used with permission (altered).

p. 27: Image by Parker Sutton (2020), used with permission (cropped).

In Conversation with Michael Marder

p. 28: Image by Samuel Ridge (2021), used with permission, incorporating portrait of Michael Marder, © Ikerbasque: Basque Foundation of Science, used with permission via author (cropped & altered).

p. 32–33: Selected artworks from *The Chernobyl Herbarium* by Anaïs Tondeur (2011–2016), used with permission.

It's Not Easy Bein' Green

p. 37: Garden Color Table image from Carl Ludwig Willdenow, *Grundriss der Kräuterkunde zu Vorlesungen* (Haude und Spener, 1792). Courtesy Max Planck Institute for the History of Science Berlin, public domain.

p. 40–41: Color garden row plan and planting plan images from Gertrude Jekyll, *Colour in the Flower Garden* (London: Country Life/George Newnes, 1908), 205, 210, public domain.

p. 42: "Emerald Green" from Royal Horticultural Society & British Colour Council, *Horticultural Colour Chart* (Printed by Henry Stone and Son, Ltd., 1938–1942). Courtesy The Athenaeum of Philadelphia Collections, public domain.

Viridic Disturbance: Reprogramming the Tools of Landscape Maintenance

p. 46: Image by Michael Geffel, used with permission.

p. 48–49: Drawings by Brian Osborn, used with permission.

p. 50–51: Aerial images by Michael Geffel, used with permission.

GOD: Greenspace-Oriented Development

p. 52–56: Images courtesy of Julian Bolleter, used with permission.

In Conversation with Noam Chomsky

p. 60: Image by Jackson Plumlee (2021), used with permission.

Throwing Shade at the Green New Deal

p. 66: 40-99 12th St © Google Maps, permitted use.

p. 69: "Average trends relative to population density of settlement in income, tree cover, and racial composition for US cities" by Robert McDonald, used with permission.

p. 70: Aerial views of Houston, Texas and Queens, New York © Google Earth, permitted use.

In Conversation with Robert D. Bullard

p. 74: Portrait courtesy of Robert D. Bullard, used with permission (cropped & altered).

The Green (and Environmentally Just) New Deal

p. 84–93: Images by Jackson Plumlee (2021), used with permission.

In Conversation with Tamara Toles O'Laughlin

p. 95: Portrait by Jackie Harris, courtesy of Tamara Toles O'Laughlin, used with permission (cropped & altered).

Greenwashing a Nation

p. 100: *Greenwashing* (2021) by Leslie Jingyu Zhang, used with permission.

The Green Around the Wall

p. 106–107: Aerial image of the Great Green Wall, Senegal © Google Earth and Maxar Technologies (2021), permitted use.

p. 108: Map by Jing Cao (2021), used with permission.

p. 110: Fenced Ferlo compound aerial view by Robert Levinthal, used with permission.

p. 113: Aerial image of Ethiopian church forest © Google Earth (2020), permitted use.

Green Stuff

p. 116–117: *The Critical Zone* (2021) by Leslie Jingyu Zhang, used with permission.

p. 120–121: Sketches by Leslie Jingyu Zhang (2021), used with permission.

LA+

In this moment of seemingly compounding global crises and existential concerns about the future of the planet, LA+ pauses to consider the values and implications of speculation. How are speculative acts understood differently within specific disciplinary structures versus broader cultural perceptions? Whether employed as a means of influence, a method of production, a form of practice, a manner of inquiry, a way of seeing, or a motivating ideology, **LA+ SPECULATION** engages speculation and the speculative as world-shaping concepts worthy of deep and critical reflection. Guest edited by Christopher Marcinkoski with Javier Arpa Fernandez, contributors include:

JAVIER ARPA FERNANDEZ

MERVE BEDIR

CASEY LANCE BROWN

STUART CANDY

PAUL DOBRASZCZYK

AROUSSIAK GABRIELIAN

DAISY GINSBERG

ADRIAN HAWKER

SOUHEI IMAMU

KAREN LEWIS

MIN KYUNG LEE

CHRISTOPHER MARCINKOSKI

MPHO MATSIPA

ALEXANDRA SANKOVA

JONAH SUSSKIND

YTASHA WOMAK

OUT FALL 2022

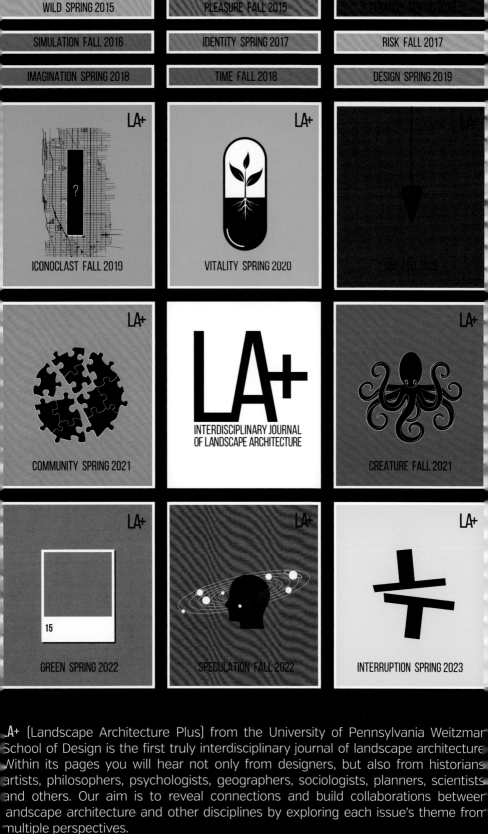

WILD SPRING 2015	PLEASURE FALL 2015	TYRANNY SPRING 2016
SIMULATION FALL 2016	IDENTITY SPRING 2017	RISK FALL 2017
IMAGINATION SPRING 2018	TIME FALL 2018	DESIGN SPRING 2019
ICONOCLAST FALL 2019	VITALITY SPRING 2020	GEO FALL 2020
COMMUNITY SPRING 2021	LA+ INTERDISCIPLINARY JOURNAL OF LANDSCAPE ARCHITECTURE	CREATURE FALL 2021
GREEN SPRING 2022	SPECULATION FALL 2022	INTERRUPTION SPRING 2023

LA+ (Landscape Architecture Plus) from the University of Pennsylvania Weitzman School of Design is the first truly interdisciplinary journal of landscape architecture. Within its pages you will hear not only from designers, but also from historians, artists, philosophers, psychologists, geographers, sociologists, planners, scientists and others. Our aim is to reveal connections and build collaborations between landscape architecture and other disciplines by exploring each issue's theme from multiple perspectives.

LA+ brings you a rich collection of contemporary thinkers and designers in two issues each year. To subscribe follow the links at WWW.LAPLUSJOURNAL.COM